THE RELIGION OF SOLIDARITY

THE RELIGION OF SOLIDARITY

The Religion of Solidarity contains fourteen incisive essays by Edward Bellamy, the nineteenth century visionary who wrote *Looking Backward*. The title essay, "The Religion of Solidarity", written when Bellamy was twenty-four, is a powerful statement on the human need for self-transcendence. "The Blind Man's World" is a bold flight of imagination in which an astronomer learns from Martians the consequences of lack of foresight, a severe handicap which intensifies the fear of death and change. "To Whom This May Come" explores the meaning and scope of friendship and intimacy amongst mind-readers. "A Republic of the Golden Rule", from *Looking Backward*, envisages the assumption of effective control of economic development through a Great Trust. "Lifelong Education", from *Equality*, considers the creative use of leisure in developing human potential.

Bellamy calls for a social system built on fraternal cooperation in "Why a New Nation?" He sets forth the basis for brotherhood in "Declaration of Principles". In "Nationalism — Principles and Purposes" he pleads for social and economic reform based upon a carefully constructed programme of nationalization, and he refines his recommendation in "Some Misconceptions of Nationalism". "Why Every Working Man Should Be a Nationalist" elucidates the benefits of true public ownership in a democracy. "The Programme of the Nationalists" points to the real significance of a radical non-violent economic revolution.

Bellamy looks forward to a Second American Revolution in "Fourth of July, 1992". He indicates the line of thinking that led him to write his famous novel in "How I Wrote 'Looking Backward'". The book concludes with his "Introduction to 'The Fabian Essays'", in which he considers Fabian socialism from a distinctively American standpoint.

THE RELIGION
OF
SOLIDARITY

EDWARD BELLAMY

CONCORD GROVE PRESS
1984

CONCORD GROVE PRESS

London   Santa Barbara   New York

First Edition: August 11, 1984

ISBN 0-88695-029-5

10 9 8 7 6 5 4 3 2 1

Printed in the United States of America

CONTENTS

THE RELIGION OF SOLIDARITY

The emotions of pleasurable melancholy and of wistful yearning produced by the prospect of a beautiful landscape are matters of universal experience, a commonplace of poetry. Upon analysis this mental experience seems to consist, if we may so express it, in a vague desire to enter into, to possess and be a part of the beauty before the eye, to come into some closer union with it than is possible consistently with the conditions of our natures. This subdued, yet intense, attraction in its disappointment produces an indefinable sadness, and it is thus that is to be explained, at least in large part, the melancholy so often observed to result from the contemplation of natural beauty. It is the disappointment of the desire after a more perfect communion. There are times in the experience of most persons of emotional temperament in which this desire (I had almost called it lust) after natural beauty amounts to a veritable orgasm. How often in the brooding warmth and stillness of summer nights, when the senses are fairly oppressed with natural beauty, and the perfumed air is laden with voluptuous solicitations, does the charm of nature grow so intense that it seems almost personal, and under its influence the senses are sublimed to an ecstasy. It is then that some almost palpable barrier seems to hold back the soul from merging with the being towards which it so passionately tends.

Sometimes with the storm wind, with moonlit waters, with wooded glens and purling brooks, with the solitary soul of mid-ocean, with lovely mountain tops, with the sunset eternally glowing over the rim of the rolling earth, with the dewy freshness of the ever virginal morning, with the new and tender pulse of spring, the thronging life, the voluptuous langour of summer, the restfulness of autumn; with these all and other innumerable aspects of nature, the human spirit sympathizes; and in this communion, despite the tinge of melancholy resulting from its imperfect consummation, finds one of its chiefest consolations and asylums.

Thus continually does the spirit in man betray affinity with nature by vague and seemingly purposeless longings to attain a more perfect sympathy with it. So far as this universal and strongly marked instinct can be distinctly interpreted, it indicates in human nature some element common with external nature towards which it is attracted, as with the attraction of a part towards a whole, and with a violence that oftentimes renders us painfully conscious of the rigorous confines of our individual organisms. This restless and discontented element is not at home in the personality, its union with it seems mechanical rather than chemical, rather of position than of essence. It is homesick for a vaster mansion than the personality affords, with an unconquerable yearning, a divine discontent, tending elsewhither.

The emotion induced in us by the monuments of bygone life are of the sort that rebel against the conditions of our organisms as persons. How often has it happened to each and every one of us to stand before some such monument of old life, some ruined specimen of ancient handiwork, some dead city or deserted site. The place is associated with the lives of generations long since mouldered away, and the gentle ghosts of their joys and sorrows seem to hover around the familiar spot, bathing it in a haze of vague reminiscence. We are conscious of a sense of loss, a feeling of deprivation, at having had no part in the skein of life that once ravelled and tangled on this very spot. We are conscious of a repining at the barrier of time that has included and shut us up in today.

The experience is very similar when, as we muse earnestly on the glories of future ages, the vision of the world to be rises before us, and we feel that in essence we belong no more to today than to yesterday and tomorrow. Such limitations appear to be arbitrary and irrelevant, impertinent, though impregnable. Hungry, not for more life, but for all the life there is, we count ourselves robbed of the days when we were not and those in which we shall not be. The reader of history surveys past ages with their processions of heroes and grand dramas as one looks upon a wide and varied country from a mountain top. What a painful incongruity is he conscious of between the soul, so easily contemporary with all time, and like an unseen presence mingling with the doings and strivings of ancient man, and his individuality weighted down to a little point of time. How trifling seems that point compared with the vast expanse seen from it, as seems his standpoint to the rapt watcher on the mountain brow, whose gaze walks unimpeded up and down the streets of a hundred villages, and follows, unfelt, the steps of the toilers in a thousand widely parted fields. The mind is conscious of a discontent that would be indignation but for its conscious impotence, that it should be thus unequal to itself. It has the aspirations of a god with the limitations of a clod, a soul that seeks to enfold and animate the universe, that takes all being for its province, and with such potential compass and desire has for its sole task the animating of one human animal in a corner of an insignificant planet.

Now who can doubt that the human soul has more in common with that life of all time and all things towards which it so eagerly goes out than with that narrow, isolated and incommodious individuality, the thrall of time and space, to which it so reluctantly, and with such a sense of belittlement and degradation, perforce returns.

Mysterious and likewise taking hold on infinite things are the emotions excited by the weird music of the Aeolian harp or the soughing of the wind in a pine forest. The music is so low, so fine and so far off that we seem to hear it by some inner ear, and we listen in involuntary awe as to the still small voice of nature. There is a sound as if the tones came from the far-off places of the universe; they intimate vast solitudes, wideness, boundless enlargement, eternal calm, eternal rhythm. In that whispered infinitude we would repose as in our proper medium; in that voice we strive to voice ourselves. We strain after the fuller life of which we recognize the sound but cannot comprehend the reality. In such moments we reach out of one plane of existence into another, and then sink back as sinks a swimmer, with grasping hands and despairing eyes turned towards the empyrean vault.

Very often in like manner must it happen to everyone, when wandering abroad at night, to feel the eyes drawn upward as by a sense of majestic, overshadowing presence. We gaze into the bottomless star-measured depths of the skies, whose infinite profounds are for the moment curtained by no cloud. The soul of the gazer is drawn through the eyes; and on and on, from star to star, still travels towards infinity. He is strange to the limitations of terrestrial things; he is out of the body. He is oppressed with the grandeur of the universal frame; its weight seems momentarily to rest upon his shoulders. But with a start and a wrench as of life from soul the personality reasserts itself; he awakes to himself, and with a temporary sense of strangeness fits himself once again to the pigmy standards about him.

The experiences which have been mentioned are but examples of the sublime, ecstatic, impersonal emotions, transcending the scope of personality or individuality, manifested by human nature, and of which the daily life of every person affords abundant instances. What, then, is the view of human nature thus suggested? Truly, one strange and awesome. On the one hand is the personal life, an atom, a grain of sand on a boundless shore, a bubble on a foam-flecked ocean, a life bearing a proportion to the mass of past, present and future life, so infinitesimal as to defy the imagination. Such is the importance of the person. On the other hand is a certain other life, as it were, a spark of the universal life, insatiable in aspiration, greedy of infinity, asserting solidarity with all things and all existence, containing the limitations of space and time and all other of the restricting conditions of the personality. On the one hand is a little group of faculties of the individual, unable even to cope with the few and simple conditions of material life, wretchedly failing, for the most part, to secure tolerable satisfaction for the physical needs of the race, and at best making slow and painful progression. On the other hand, in the soul, is a depth of divine despair over the insufficiency of this existence, already seemingly too large, and a passionate dream of immortality, the vision of a starving man whose fancy revels in full tables. Such is the estate of man, and such his dual life. As an individual he finds it a task exceeding his powers even to secure satisfactory material conditions for his physical life; as a universal he grasps at a life infinitely larger than the one he so poorly cares for. This dual life of man, personal and impersonal, as an individual and as a universal, goes far to explain the riddle of human nature and human destiny.*

Since it is a common error to imagine the impersonal consciousness as a thing altogether vague and shadowy, while the personal consciousness or soul life is the only real and substantial

* Here several pages of the manuscript seem to be missing.

hold on existence, it will be well by way of correcting this notion to advert to some of the continual instances in our daily spiritual experience in which we closely approximate the impersonal mood. For instance, in the degree in which we realize beauty of any sort we approach the impersonal condition and obtain a hint of the mode of our impersonal consciousness. It is only when we can say that we forget ourselves and in a certain mystic way seem to share the life of the thing admired that we taste the pure and high felicity of a perfect realization of a perfect sense of beauty. It is in measure as we are rapt out of ourselves into this mood of impersonal consciousness that we are sublimed by the impulses of self-devotion and attain the grand experience of enthusiasm. Those mental states which we call the noblest, broadest and most inspired, the most intense and satisfying of our psychical felicities, in fine all those emotions and moods by which we are greater than our personalities, and which constitute the larger and far more essential part of our lives — all these are but the activity of the greater self, the impersonal consciousness within us.

The fact of consciousness most clearly witnessing to impersonality of the soul is that, whereas the animal functions are constant quantities, varying only with their supplies of nutriment and stimulus, the soul is most inconstant, as if it were continually coming and going, now dull and lifeless, now again vivified, glowing, expanding as it is touched with some inspiration of enthusiasm or some sentiment of sympathy with the larger life. I know of nothing with which to compare this continual flux and reflux but to the phenomena presented by the northern lights, which on a winter night now irradiate the whole vault of the heavens with torrents of light, throwing their spray over the earth, and again sinking away to the horizon, leaving the sky black and dead. So is the soul, ever rising and falling, wavering, undulating, ever glowing and fading, ebbing and flowing as from some eternal reservoir. "The wind bloweth where it listeth, and thou hearest the sound thereof, but canst not tell whence it cometh, and whither it goeth." So is the soul of man born again in every fresh inbreathing of the soul of solidarity.

In view of such phenomena, where is the claim of the personality of the soul, and its sufficient, self-comprehending consciousness? I can as easily imagine the little inlets of the ocean coast boasting that the tides that daily throb through them are spontaneous with them, as a man boasting that these tides and tempests of the soul arise within his own personality, and do not rather come from the uttermost parts of the universe.

Genius is the vivid partaking of the soul of solidarity. It is essentially impersonal in its manifestations; the personality of the subject is in suspense. To be possessed of his genius, the man must be unconscious of his personality; he must be beside himself, even as the Delphic priestess was required to be before the oracle spoke through her. We can but conclude, then, from all this testimony of our own experiences, that unconsciousness of personality or impersonal consciousness does not imply a vague and shadowy mode of being, but rather a stronger, intenser pulse of feeling than is obtainable in the most vigorous assertion of the personality. Individuality, personality, partiality, is segregation, is partition, is confinement; is, in fine, a prison, and happy are we if its walls grow not wearisome ere our seventy years' sentence expires.

To pursue this argument, it appears to me (the testimony of his own consciousness is the only evidence that any person can receive in this matter) that the last effort in introspection discloses in the penetralia of the soul an impersonal consciousness. Tracing to its awful source the river of life within us, what do we find it, we who claim so confidently to be personal, self-comprehending, self-complete entities? Will anyone be so bold as to say that he can fathom, even in untranslatable emotions, that fount of being whence wells the sense of existence? Ponder well. Do we not feel ourselves at once a part of, and external to, the last impregnable consciousness, that citadel of being? We are at once it and of it, itself, yet not all of it. In fine, it is impersonal. It is the witness of our life, and we are the witness of its life. With nothing are we more identical, yet it is as awful to us as infinity, unspeakable as God. Ask for no heavens to open nor firmament to dissolve that you may be left faced with God and see the sum end of things. Steadfastly look into the well of your own life and know the powerlessness of human tongues to express its endless depths, its boundless contents. Ere you think of any other infinity, fathom and compass that, and be prepared to learn that there is but one problem in the universe, and that is the nature of the soul, which is one in you and in all things.

Moods of insight visit us all, in which our natures go deepening on and up, until we feel we are infinity within ourselves and turn back shuddering from its brink. The pettiness of the personality comes in sharp contrast with these stupendous and labyrinthine reaches of the soul, forming a bizarre and glaring opposition, seeming inscrutable, and impressing us with a strange sense of mystery and self-ignorance. But when we come to regard the profound within us as the presence of the All of being, with which we are far more deeply and indissolubly identical than with our individualities, to which the contrasted pettinesses pertain, we cease to mingle the two strains of emotions but act in one and rest in the other.

There are few of an introspective habit who are not haunted with a certain very definite sense of a second soul, an inner serene and passionless ego, which regards the experiences of the individual with a superior curiosity, as it were, a half pity. It is especially in moments of the deepest anguish or of the maddest gaiety, that is, in the intensest strain of the individuality, that we are conscious of the dual soul as of a presence serenely regarding from another plane of being the agitated personality. It is at such times as that we become, not by force of argument, but by spontaneous experience, strictly subjective to ourselves, that is, the individuality becomes objective to the universal soul, that eternal subjective. The latter regards the former as a god is conceived to look upon man, in an attitude passionless, disinterested, yet pitiful. Often does it happen in scenes of revellry or woe that we are thus suddenly translated, looking down calmly upon our passion-wrung selves, and then as with an effort, once more enduring the weeds or tinsel of our personal estates. At such times we say that we have been out of ourselves; but in reality we have been into ourselves; we have only just realized the greater half of our being. We have momentarily lived in the infinite part of our being, a region ever open and waiting for us, if we will but frequent its highlands. We call such an experience abnormal; it should be normal.

We dwell needlessly in the narrow grotto of the individual life, counting as strange, angelic visitants the sunbeams that struggle thither, not being able to believe that the upper universe is our world to live in, the grotto of the personality a mere workshop. We are content to conjecture from occasional intuitions a world that we should constantly recognize. The half-conscious god that is man is called to recognize his divine parts. The soul then is what it would be. It has the infinity it craves. We restrict ourselves. Spread your wings; you will reach no horizon. Cast out the lead; it will strike no bottom. Our little wells are filled from this eternal life; our souls are not islands in the void, but peninsulas forming one continent of life within the universe. It is man's own indolence that will inhabit but one corner of the open universe, a corner of himself. Let him assume his birthright, and live out, live up, in others, in the past, in the future, in nature, in God. There are no barriers to the soul but such as sense-bound fancy imagines. When Thales enunciated the maxim "Know thyself", he propounded a problem not to be solved, for the human soul is continuous with it. The dual existence of man is at once infinite and infinitesimal and particular.

I do not assert that the higher universal life is at once realizable by merely resolving thereon. Like his present endowment of mental faculties which man has slowly and painfully evolved since the savage state, so the full consciousness and active enjoyment of the universal soul will be slow and difficult in being realized. Potentially, indeed, the universal life is manifesting itself within us by countless unmistakable signs, but it is in the mind of Shakespeare as in the cave dwellers. It remains for us, by culture of our spiritual cognitions, by education, drawing forth of our partially latent universal instincts, to develop into a consciousness as coherent, definite and indefeasible as that of our individual life, the all-identical life of the universe within us. Nor is this tendency of the human soul to a more perfect realization of its solidarity with the universe, by the development of instincts partly or wholly latent, altogether a theory. It is already an observed fact, a matter of history. I would call attention to the fact that sentimental love of the beautiful and sublime in nature, the charm which mountains, sea and landscape so potently exercise upon the modern mind through a subtle sense of sympathy, is a comparatively modern and recent growth of the human mind. The ancients knew, or at least say, nothing of it. It is a curious fact that in no classical author are to be found any allusions to a class of emotions and sentiments that take up such large space in modern literature. It is almost within a century, in fact, that this susceptibility of the soul seems to have been developed. It is not, therefore, surprising that its language should still be vague. I am sure that much of the unrest and reaching out after the infinite, which is the peculiar characteristic of this age, is the result of this new sense. If culture can add such a province as this to human nature within a century, it is surely not visionary to count on a still more complete future development of the same group of subtle psychical faculties.

The influence of an acceptance of the view of life which has now been outlined should not be to breed a discontent with ourselves as individuals. The personality should not be contemned, should not be worn with half-heartedness and repining. It is dignified in being the channel, the expression, of the universal. In this view it has as sound a right of being as the universal itself. Its joys we do well to push to the uttermost, interpreting them by the universal and thus lending them sublimity. Its sorrows we should not, on the other hand, contemn nor bear too heavily, but tenderly pity from the higher plane the bereavements of the individual, accepting their monitions towards the universal, the all-pervading life. In that lofty, overlooking region, in that supernal, passionless atmosphere, learn to make a home and build there an everlasting habitation, whither to retire when the personal life is overclouded, its windows darkened, and all its functions palsied with the bitterness of disappointment and the anguish of bereavement.

Perhaps the relations of the universal and individual lives may be more distinctly brought before the mind by imagining them under the types, respectively, of the centripetal and centrifugal forces as illustrated in celestial mechanics. The instinct of universal solidarity, of the identity of our lives with all life, is the centripetal force which binds together in certain orbits all orders of beings. In fine, the instinct of solidarity in the moral universe correlates with the attraction of gravitation in the material world.

The fact of individuality with its tendency to particularizations is the centrifugal force which hinders the universal fusion, the natural result of the unimpeded operation of the centripetal force, and preserves the variety in unity which seems the destined condition of being. Thus these mutually balancing forces play each its necessary part, and each we may suppose to be an absolute fact. It is the instinct of personality which leads man, weary of exploring the universe and striving to grasp the relations of it to other orders of being, to take refuge in the bundle of mental and physical experiences which he calls himself, as the only thing of which he is absolutely sure, the sole rock in the midst of an illimitable ocean. It is this instinct which at times sends him off, as it were, on a tangent from his orbit, in defiance of the centripetal instinct of solidarity in mad self-assertion, in wild rebellion against subordination or coherency with anything.

It is this vicious habit of regarding the personality as an ultimate fact instead of a mere temporary effection of the universal that at times overcomes the mind with a sense of utter and unnecessary isolation, of inexpressible loneliness, of a great gulf between the successive personalities of a single individuality and all others. It is this instinct which lends its horror of quiet darkness to death, for death is the dissolution of the individuality and the enfranchisement of the atom of the universal which has been segregated in it. On the other hand, it is the instinct of solidarity, however misconstrued or unconfessed, which lends mere consciousness of greatness, otherwise unaccountable, a sense of majesty utterly, nay ludicrously, beyond that which is warranted by the proportion of his personality to the sum of personalities. It is this which makes a man, however good his will, unable to isolate himself from the general frame of things and to conceive of the universe as going on without him. The universe never did and never will go on without him. It is this which renders it all essential for his comfort, to feel that he is acting a part of some universal plan or frame of things, thus making some sort of religion or philosophy indispensable to him and rendering the notion of unconnected, isolated action abhorrent to his soul. The opposition in human nature of the two ideas of solidarity and personality may be further illustrated by describing as an expression of the former the sense of the sublime, of the grand, or whatever may be called the instinct of infinity, and on the other hand as an expression of the personality, the desire of being circumscribed, shut in and bounded, the aversion to vague limitations, the sense of coziness (if I may venture to give a philosophical meaning to that peculiar word) or what may be called the instinct of finity. To the latter class of feelings the former seems to open an abstract, unreal, remote and frigid cloudland, utterly repugnant to its own warm and cheerful, if confined, precincts.

In turn, the instinct of finity to its opposite seems synonymous with pettiness, with infinitesimality, suggestive of a mean, base and narrow scope, a low-lying, sensuous atmosphere. Their opposition, whereof the mental experience of every reader will have furnished abundant instances, is another testimony of consciousness to the dual constitution of the human soul.

Much sorrow of man comes from his efforts, in imperfect understanding of his own nature, to crowd his universal life into his personal experience, to grasp and realize with the functions of the finite the suggestions of the infinite. He is thus led to make too much of the joys and sorrows and circumstances of the person. Conscious of universal instincts, his mistake lies in expecting the experiences of the individual to be of like scope. He would have the relationships of the individual endowed with the attributes of the universal. Conscious fully of the individual life, his constant effort is to express, as it were, universal instincts in terms of the individuality. No wonder human joy has such an undertone of sadness, and all the concern of the individual life seems but vanity of vanities. It is the mistake of requiring the finite to meet the criterion of the infinite. The joys and sorrows of the individual are adapted to its scope. To seek in them any completer significance is to tempt disappointment. What man complains of as an incurable incongruity between his soul and its external surroundings and the scope by them imposed is in the stricter truth an incongruity between the two aspects of his own nature. The remedy is ceasing to confuse them and rendering to each the things of each.

We should ever interpret the finite in us by the infinite, but the infinite by the finite, never. For instance, if we interpret love as a partial realization under the hindering conditions of individuality of that complete fusion of souls which is the centripetal tendency of the universal instincts, we sublime our passions, so that an experience of the individual life becomes an eloquent revelation of the universal. But if loving we dream of such a union, but dream of it as if consistent with self-assertion and the preservation of our personalities, we fall into the absurdity of interpreting the one by the many, the universal by the individual. Personalities cannot absorb each other; their essence is diversity. For our personalities, therefore, we cannot expect a perfect intimacy free from all incompatibility and antagonism, but may only solace ourselves with occasional realization of an ecstasy of ineffable tenderness, transitory glimpses of that oneness of our universal parts which overarches and includes all individual diversities. Looking for a perfect outward harmony and fitting together personalities, even of those best adapted and most passionately attached, we shall ever meet with bitter disappointment, but in the higher plane of this larger life we can always realize that fusion and identity that is the heart of all love.

So, too, in that other great experience of the individual, bereavement by death, if we are able to interpret the many by the one, the individual by the universal, we find great consolation for the death of a friend in reflecting that he has but given up that part of him in which he was diverse and separate from us, that is, his personality, to exist henceforth, as far as we know, wholly in the part in which he is one with us and one with all. Truly, not with our bodily passions can we sympathize with his new life. He no longer bears those traits of personality by which these were roused. Our body and the physical sympathies born of it must needs be bereaved; also those mental traits (equally peculiarities of the individuality) which formerly sympathized with the dead. All these are mortal and miss the mortal parts of the dead. For this bereavement there is no remedy, and it is worthy the tribute of tears. But our real life, the indefeasible consciousness of being, the life of solidarity, which, connected with the body, so transcended its conditions, we may legitimately believe to survive its decay, nay, perhaps, to be then first set free by that decay, and by this higher life at once in us and in all, we are united to the living and to the dead. For this life of solidarity there is neither past nor present, mortality nor immortality, but life ever present, which dons and doffs the countless and varied guises of individuality as one puts on and takes off his garments.

As individuals, then, we have nothing in common with the dead. In that attitude we cannot commune with them, but as universals we are one with them. Nothing should greatly shake those who have their foundations so deeply fixed. But if we reverse this philosophy and interpret the universal by the individual, then, indeed, our plight is pitiable. We are seeking to super-add the universal to the individual, the infinite to the finite, and for result have an incongruous, unthinkable conception more fruitful in vague questioning and in repining than in belief. Claiming a most undesirable immortality for personal traits that even in this life in the course of a few years so utterly change, we cannot consent to regard as perishable those idiosyncrasies, those mental squints and biases, which by the variation of defects are the only marks of intellectualities. It seems as if without these we should lose our identity. And so indeed we should lose our identity as individuals, so factitious, unsubstantial, easily lost a thing is that, a thing of an earmark, more or less.

Who has not often felt in sudden shocks of feeling as if the sense of personal identity, i.e., sense of his connection with his particular individuality, were slipping from him? To such as recall similar experiences, and surely all persons must, they will supply the need of argument in convincing them that the personality is a very precarious possession, held by a thread, which will sustain but a feeble strain. The tendency of the mind to ecstasies, trances and similar suspensions of the sense of personal identity, at times when the body is in a morbid state, as well as the perfectly healthful exaltations of enthusiasm, are additional illustrations of the same truth. I speak of well-known psychological phenomena, and but parenthetically advert to them in claiming their testimony to the accidental connections of the soul with the personality; the latter being, as it were, attached for fair-weather purposes only, by joints that show their seams in every strain of the machine.

To return to the argument: in losing our personal identity, we should become conscious of our other, our universal identity, the identity of a universal solidarity — not losable in the universe, for it fills it. Let us then play with our individual lives as with toys, building them into beautiful forms and delighting ourselves in so brave a game; for have we not our true life, our impregnable citadel of being, as safe from the mishaps of the individual as the serene stars are safe from the earth's uproar and confusion? Be not careful, then, of your goings and doings. Be not deluded into magnifying their importance. Live with a certain calm abandon, a serene and generous recklessness. The things of the individual are at best but trifles, the rents of tinsel in the garment of a day. Be not hard or mean in spending your lives. Be not miserly in hoarding them. What parsimony could seem so supremely laughable in the eyes of onlooking God? It is like the demented millionaire who saves his crusts. The individuality is of so little importance, of such trifling scope, that it should matter little to us what renunciations of its things we make, what inequalities, what deprivations in its experiences we endure. We should hold our lives loosely, and not with the convulsive grip of one who counts personal life his all. The workman does not sacrifice himself to his tools, so should we not seek to serve the individual, which is the serf of the universal, by any sacrifice of those universal instincts, whereof the chief is unselfishness, which constitute true morality.

Our lives are comedy. In the universal there is no tragedy, and in the realm of the individual the experiences are too trifling for the dignity of tragedy. Melancholy and grief, fate or accident, never triumph over the true life of man, only over that transient and unimportant phase of it known as the personality. Justly regarded, human life is a delightful game of passions and calculating, superior in interest to chess on account of the sense of partial identity with the personalities which serve as puppets, while at the same time that sense of identity, at least to a philosopher's mind, is so incomplete as to prevent the interest from attaining a painful degree of intensity.

Seeing there is in every human being a soul common in nature with all other souls, but in a measure isolated by the conditions of individuality, it is easy to understand the origin of that cardinal motive of human life, which is a tendency and a striving to absorb or be absorbed in or united with other lives and all life. This passion for losing ourselves in others or for absorbing them into ourselves, which rebels against individuality as an impediment, is then the expression of the greatest law of solidarity. So long as the particle of this life of solidarity within us is hindered by individual conditions from merging with the rest, that is, with the all, so long will desire and the pathos of its partial disappointment be an underlying fact of human nature. It is the operation of this law in great and low things, in the love of men for women and for each other, for the race, for nature, and for those great ideas which are the symbols of solidarity, that has ever made up the web and woof of human passion. Love between individuals is the attraction between kindred particles, but the greatest of all loves, at once the most enthusiastic, the most sustaining, the most insatiable love of loves, is that of an individual for his remnant, the universe. This is the love of God by whatever name men may choose to call it.

The manner in which love asserts itself between individuals is illustrative of its genesis in the law of solidarity. It is the nature of our souls to fuse together, for they are one, but by the conditions of individuality, the particle in each one of us is, as it were, fenced about and shut into itself. There it pines in loneliness, breeding infinite discontent and prompting all manner of godlike movings, which mightily disquiet the individual as to what may be the nature of this inmate which spurns in such lordly fashion surroundings which fit the individual so well. It holds to reason that the restless soul will take advantage of any relaxation in the rigour of the conditions of the individuality to flow out towards its fellow particles and essay fusion with them. This relaxation may result either from a correlation of the physical or mental faculties of individuals, or it may result from habitual association and the mutual accommodation of faculties resulting therefrom.

The sexual relation is the greatest example of that physical correlation which, approximating the individualities and relaxing the rigour of their natural attitude of mutual antagonism and exclusiveness, affords an opportunity for the confluence in at least a partial sympathy of the roles of lovers, and the bliss resulting from the consciousness of even this imperfect union is a proof of the common essence of souls. But after all, how imperfect is this union, even when helped to the utmost by physical conditions. You find a woman at whose face you never tire of gazing, with a desire miraculously filling a full heart fuller. Fortune gives her to your arms, and the fruit of physical satiety has been yours. But is your desire satisfied? Can it thus be other than mocked? It is herself, her soul, her utter life, which you would absorb, into which you would be absorbed, and with which you would be one. There is a lust of soul for soul dwarfing the lust of body for body, as the universal dwarfs the individual; a lust insatiable, a passion hopeless yet entrancing, sweeter in desire than all others in consummation. The poet lover finds not much difference whether the bodily embraces of his mistress be granted or denied him. He knows that nothing could satisfy his passion, and counts the physical possession a thing almost indifferent to the attainment of his dreams.

Thus much of the hunger of souls for each other is born of the physical correlation of the individualities. But such a sympathy may spring as well from a mental correlation which is only of the individual. Such an adaptation of mind to mind that their natural antagonisms are relaxed produces this form of partial realization of soul solidarity. Intellectual companionships are of this nature. But there is another kind of soul sympathy and tendency to oneness. I refer to that which springs from family life, that which endears with an altogether peculiar and intimate endearment brothers and sisters, the members of one household, from childhood; this, too, without any apparent original correlation, mental or physical, between the persons. Nevertheless, the correlation exists, only here it is the result of the attrition of habitual intercourse. As the roughest surfaces, by dint of constantly rubbing against each other, become at last smooth or adapt their qualities to each other's forms, so persons associated in the close and constant relationships of family life become at last so fitted to each other that their souls naturally flow together. This is the genesis of family love. Nay, it is this super-induced correlation of habit that lends an element, frequently the largest element, to post-nuptial love. It is the gentle work of time that mends the blunders of the blind god, and binds closely individuals with but small original physical or mental correlation.

Besides the physical correlation between the sexes, there is also a sex of intellect, thus affording twofold correlation, a cord not easily broken. And when the mutual confluence of souls thus induced has been perfected by the added influence of long habits of intimacy, we have an example of the most complete realization of soul fusion that intercourse permits. It is not to be supposed, then, that the difficulty we find in sympathizing with some persons arises from lack of soul in them, but rather from lack of mental or physical correlation between us. Paradoxical as it may seem, the most perfect lover given us on earth is our own lover, not because of special adaptation of his soul to ours, for the essence of all souls is one, but by reason of our special mutual mental and physical adaptation, which, relaxing the mutual antagonisms of our personalities, allows the spirits to fuse. Individualities may or may not match well. Here is room for choice, but souls always match, for they are inhalations of one breath, tongues of one flame.

It seems that at some times the sympathy of solidarity asserts itself in connection with states of physical exaltation, and sometimes quite independently of them. Thus, narcotics, intoxicants and the natural stimulants of beauty, music, a soft bland air, perfume, often produce singly or unitedly a state very favourable to this psychical experience. They are thus influential, I suppose, by virtue of relaxing the rigour of individual conditions, as it were, laying the petty, petulant instincts of the personality under a spell. This must be the manner of their operation, for it seems that the langour of the faculties resulting from extreme exhaustion is equally favourable to the same psychical experience. I conclude, then, that the physical condition favourable to it is that of suspension of the sense of wants and requirements of the body, which end is attained either from their satisfaction or their torpor from narcotics or from exhaustion. But, as above intimated, the instincts of universal solidarity also assert themselves quite independently of physical conditions, responding to direct moral appeal, to eloquence of speech or written word, or to the description of beauty or sublimity.

The union of the physical influences described with those of a more purely moral nature produces more remarkable effects than either class alone; as, when the inspiration of martial music, combining with the instinct of nationalism (which is one of the soldierly forms of solidarity), the heart of the soldier melts in a happy rapture of self-devotion. He is impatient to throw his life away and rejoices in his body as a sacrifice which he can make for his country, even as the priest rejoices in a victim for the altar of his god.

It is this mixture of the physical and moral influences that gives its wonderful power to music combined with religious service. Room fails me for the crowding illustrations of this point. The beautiful sublimities and infinities of nature are, however, the most constant reminders to the instinct of solidarity. The sky and the sea are two types of infinity that should always suffice to recall us from absorption in the individual side of our nature. They are the material symbols of the soul's infinity, and as the piety of the Romanist revives at the sight of the crucifix, so should the religion of universal solidarity stir freshly in us whenever our eyes are raised to the bottomless vault of heaven or scan the unbounded sea. In the religion of solidarity is found the only rational philosophy of the moral instincts. Unselfishness, self-sacrifice, is the essence of morality. On the theory of ultimate individualities, unselfishness is madness; but on the theory of the dual life, of which the life of solidarity is abiding and that of the individual transitory, unselfishness is but the sacrifice of the lesser self to the greater self, an eminently rational and philosophical proceeding *per se,* and entirely regardless of ulterior considerations. The moral intuitions which impel to self-sacrifice are the instincts of the life of solidarity asserting themselves against the instincts of the individuality. Hence the majesty beyond appeal in their monitions. As the individuality has its appetites and passions, so the universal life has its passions of self-debasement, its rebellious, self-torturing sympathies, its generous longings. The individuality would always sacrifice other individualities to itself, but the soul of solidarity within us is equally indifferent to all individualities, having in view only the harmony of the universal life as its exigencies require, impels now the sacrifice of my individuality, now of yours. Perhaps it may well be said here that unselfishness according to the religion of solidarity is as inconsistent with undue self-abnegation as with undue self-assertion. It requires in all cases the fulfilment of the instinct of the whole, which may indifferently coincide with the assertion or abnegation of any particular individuality. A bias in favour of altruism is as obnoxious to its principles as the contrary bias in favour of self.

If the thought occur that the soul of solidarity so removed from all affectations of individuality can scarcely be supposed to inspire principles of individual conduct, it suffices to remember that the soul of solidarity is primarily an instinct of an identity of oneness. In the inorganic world we may imagine it as the attraction of cohesion. In the various orders of animated nature it appears in the shape of varied laws of mutual independence and attractions. Manifested in men it takes the form of loyalty or patriotism, philanthropy or sympathy. According to the different forms of individualizations which it animates, the soul of solidarity variously but invariably exerts its centripetal tendency, but its law is always to bind the members of each order first to their own system, and then to the sum of all systems, even as in celestial mechanics the force of gravitation first and most evidently binds the single systems together, and then sends all systems alike revolving about some great single centre. Thus it is that men are conscious first of the solidarity of the race, then more dimly of that of the universe.

The secret of many diversities in human character consists in the comparative development of the universal and individual life. Poets, mystics, dreamers, seers and all of that ilk are marked by an overpowering sense of their element of universal soul. On the other hand, men of affairs, energetic, self-asserting, pushing people have in general their universal instincts imperfectly developed. Given great powers, of such men are made Napoleons and Caesars. Yet such as these are great in the individual plane only. He who has but glimmering visions of the universal stands on a plane infinitely above them. They are great as individuals, a sort of pigmy greatness not to be desired.

All human knowledge consists in the apprehension of differences and resemblances, discords and harmonies of the universe, in analysis and synthesis, in distinction and generalization. The former or analysing faculties pertain peculiarly to natures strongly developed on the individual side. The latter, the synthetical faculty, the disposition to perceive harmonies and unities rather than discords and differences, is characteristic of natures more open on the side towards the universe, in which the instincts of general solidarity are more vivid. What we call talent exists with characters in which the individual side is predominant; but genius, which is but a vivid realization of the universal, is the dower only of natures dominated by impulses from that side. The genius is never self-conscious while the afflatus is upon him. He is beside himself and thus delivers his oracle of the universal, himself a priest of the infinite.

Telescopic and microscopic are the two windows through which man looks out, the former opening on the infinite, the latter on the infinitesimal. Neither window should be obscured or ignored. Not the Indian Buddhist in ecstatic contemplation, seeking to merge himself in God in disregard of his active status as an individual; not the self-seeker in the insanity of individualism, concentrating his being in microscopic activities (equally microscopic whether they concern faggots or empires, since they are pursued in the spirit of individualism); neither of these is the ideal man. But rather he whose spirit dwells in the stars and in all time, but whose hands are as deft with the most menial as with the mightiest tasks through which the promptings of the soul of solidarity can find expression, who turns his hands with equal readiness to founding empires and to washing beggars' feet, holding all tasks in equal honour, since with him the infinite motive utterly overshadows the deed itself, at best infinitesimal in all questions of its success or failure. It is indeed a pitiable endeavour that seeks to satisfy the craving for grandeur and boundlessness inherent in the soul by piling Pelion on Ossa in achievements undertaken in the spirit of personal aggrandizement. Alexander, thus seeking to fill the void within him, must needs eternally weep for new worlds to conquer, although forever conquering. Yet there is a possibility, a secret of satisfying, even this hunger. But it is not by quantity of deeds, but by quality of motives, the spirit in which the deeds are done. The largest deeds of the individual must forever remain infinitesimal, but the spirit of the meanest deed may be infinite, all-satisfying. Poor Alexander had his problem by the wrong end. As individuals we are indeed limited to a narrow spot in today, but as universalists we inherit all time and space. More and more to make the larger life the true and central, the individual inferior and accidental, be the end of our philosophy.

There is a conscious solidarity of the universe towards the intuition of which we must struggle, that it may become to us, not a logical abstraction, but a felt and living fact. As individuals we shall never be complete. The completest man lacks the completion of the rest of the universe. Part, then, with the feeling of the externalibility to the universe, which, coupled with the sense of utter ignorance and powerlessness, is so full of despair. Believe that your sympathy with infinite being, infinite extension, infinite variety, is a pledge of identity. Above all, disabuse your mind of the notion that this life is essentially incomplete and preliminary in its nature and destined to issue in some final state. For this notion there is no warrant in reason nor in proper interpretation of intuitions. Time is not a vestibule of eternity, but a part of it. We are now living our immortal lives. This present life is its own perfect consummation, its own reason and excuse. The life of infinite range that our intuitions promise us lies even now open round about us. The avenues leading to it, the vistas opening upon it, are those universal instincts that continually stir us, and which if followed out would lead us thither. It is our own dull lack of faith that causes us to regard them as of no present but only of future significance, that places our heaven ever in some dim land of tomorrow, instead of all about us in the eternal present.

The individuality dies; the soul never. It is inconceivable how it could taste an immortality more perfect than it now enjoys. Nor can a life of wider scope be imagined than that the soul already takes hold of by its universal instincts, and which by the culture of those instincts even now, more and infinitely more, realizable by us. But as the Christian believer strives that he may enter into the mystical kingdom of heaven, so also the infinite enlargement of life spoken of awaits only those who strive after it in a like spirit.

In the universal instincts within us we are given sure and certain lodestones that we must interpret by meditation and follow with enthusiasm and faith, whereof the steadily increasing force and clearness of our intuitions will afford constant justification. Surely a more engaging mode of life than its own infinite enlargement we could not set before us. What respect can be claimed for aspirations after other forms and higher grades of life by those who are too dull to imagine the present infinite potentialities of their souls? When will men learn to interpret their intuitions of heaven and infinite things in the present, instead of forever in the future?

Comments by Edward Bellamy, added to the manuscript in 1887

I should like this paper to be read to me when I am about to die. This tribute I may render without conceit to the boy of twenty-four who wrote it.

This paper, which was written in 1874, when I was twenty-four, represents the germ of what has been ever since my philosophy of life. This paper, which I never offered for publication, is crude and redundant in style and contains some obvious defects in ratiocinations, lost links which I could now supply, but I have never cared to do so. I could say also much more on the same theme; I could draw from my later experiences, expand it into a volume. This maybe I shall sometime do, should I continue in this state of existence. But I have always been slow to publish my opinion concerning these supreme matters. Yet by this time I begin to feel that this is my ripe judgement of life, and that I should be justified in putting it forth as such.

THE BLIND MAN'S WORLD

The narrative to which this note is introductory was found among the papers of the late Professor S. Erastus Larrabee and, as an acquaintance of the gentleman to whom they were bequeathed, I was requested to prepare it for publication. This turned out a very easy task, for the document proved of so extraordinary a character that, if published at all, it should obviously be without change. It appears that the professor did really, at one time in his life, have an attack of vertigo, or something of the sort, under circumstances similar to those described by him, and to that extent his narrative may be founded on fact. How soon it shifts from that foundation, or whether it does at all, the reader must conclude for himself. It appears certain that the professor never related to anyone, while living, the stranger features of the experience here narrated, but this might have been merely from fear that his standing as a man of science would be thereby injured.

THE PROFESSOR'S NARRATIVE

At the time of the experience of which I am about to write, I was professor of astronomy and higher mathematics at Abercrombie College. Most astronomers have a specialty, and mine was the study of the planet Mars, our nearest neighbour but one in the sun's little family. When no important celestial phenomena in other quarters demanded attention, it was on the ruddy disc of Mars that my telescope was oftenest focussed. I was never weary of tracing the outlines of its continents and seas, its capes and islands, its bays and straits, its lakes and mountains. With intense interest I watched from week to week of the Martial winter the advance of the polar ice-cap towards the equator, and its corresponding retreat in the summer, testifying across the gulf of space as plainly as written words to the existence on that orb of a climate like our own. A specialty is always in danger of becoming an infatuation, and my interest in Mars, at the time of which I write, had grown to be more than strictly scientific. The impression of the nearness of this planet, heightened by the wonderful distinctness of its geography as seen through a powerful telescope, appeals strongly to the imagination of the astronomer. On fine evenings I used to spend hours, not so much critically observing as brooding over its radiant surface, till I could almost persuade myself that I saw the breakers dashing on the bold shore of Kepler Land, and heard the muffled thunder of avalanches descending the snowclad mountains of Mitchell. No earthly landscape had the charm to hold my gaze of that far-off planet, whose oceans, to the unpractised eye, seem but darker, and its continents lighter, spots and bands.

Astronomers have agreed in declaring that Mars is undoubtedly habitable by beings like ourselves, but, as may be supposed, I was not in a mood to be satisfied with considering it merely habitable. I allowed no sort of question that it was inhabited. What manner of beings these inhabitants might be I found a fascinating speculation. The variety of types appearing in mankind even on this small Earth makes it most presumptuous to assume that the denizens of different planets may not be characterized by diversities far profounder. Wherein such diversities, coupled with a general resemblance to man, might consist, whether in mere physical differences or in different mental laws, in the lack of certain of the great passional motors of men or the possession of quite others, were weird themes of never-failing attractions for my mind. The El Dorado visions with which the virgin mystery of the New World inspired the early Spanish explorers were tame and prosaic compared with the speculations which it was perfectly legitimate to indulge when the problem was the conditions of life on another planet.

It was the time of the year when Mars is most favourably situated for observation, and, anxious not to lose an hour of the precious season, I had spent the greater part of several successive nights in the observatory. I believed that I had made some original observations as to the trend of the coast of Kepler Land between Lagrange Peninsula and Christie Bay, and it was to this spot that my observations were particularly directed.

On the fourth night other work detained me from the observing chair till after midnight. When I had adjusted the instrument and took my first look at Mars, I remember being unable to restrain a cry of admiration. The planet was fairly dazzling. It seemed nearer and larger than I had ever seen it before, and its peculiar ruddiness more striking. In thirty years of observations, I recall, in fact, no occasion when the absence of exhalations in our atmosphere has coincided with such cloudlessness in that of Mars as on that night.

I could plainly make out the white masses of vapour at the opposite edges of the lighted disc, which are the mists of its dawn and evening. The snowy mass of Mount Hall over against Kepler Land stood out with wonderful clearness, and I could unmistakably detect the blue tint of the ocean of De La Rue, which washes its base — a feat of vision often, indeed, accomplished by star-gazers, though I had never done it to my complete satisfaction before.

I was impressed with the idea that if I ever made an original discovery in regard to Mars, it would be on that evening, and I believed that I should do it. I trembled with mingled exultation and anxiety, and was obliged to pause to recover my self-control. Finally, I placed my eye to the eyepiece, and directed my gaze upon the portion of the planet in which I was especially interested. My attention soon became fixed and absorbed much beyond my wont when observing, and that itself implied no ordinary degree of abstraction. To all mental intents and purposes I was on Mars. Every faculty, every susceptibility of sense and intellect, seemed gradually to pass into the eye and become concentrated in the act of gazing. Every atom of nerve and will-power combined in the strain to see a little, and yet a little, and yet a little clearer, farther, deeper.

The next thing I knew I was on the bed that stood in a corner of the observing room, half-raised on an elbow, and gazing intently at the door. It was broad daylight. Half a dozen men, including several of the professors and a doctor from the village, were around me. Some were trying to make me lie down, others were asking me what I wanted, while the doctor was urging me to drink some whiskey. Mechanically repelling their offices, I pointed to the door and ejaculated, "President Byxbee — coming", giving expression to the one idea which my dazed mind at that moment contained. And sure enough, even as I spoke the door opened, and the venerable head of the college, somewhat blown with climbing the steep stairway, stood on the threshold. With a sensation of prodigious relief, I fell back on my pillow.

It appeared that I had swooned while in the observing chair the night before, and had been found by the janitor in the morning, my head fallen forward on the telescope, as if still observing, but my body cold, rigid, pulseless and apparently dead.

In a couple of days I was all right again, and should soon have forgotten the episode but for a very interesting conjecture which had suggested itself in connection with it. This was nothing less than that, while I lay in that swoon, I was in a conscious state outside and independent of the body, and in that state received impressions and exercised perceptive powers. For this extraordinary theory I had no other evidence than the fact of my knowledge in the moment of awaking that President Byxbee was coming up the stairs. But slight as this clue was, it seemed to me unmistakable in its significance. That knowledge was certainly in my mind on the instant of arousing from the swoon. It certainly could not have been there before I fell into the swoon. I must therefore have gained it in the meantime; that is to say, I must have been in a conscious, percipient state while my body was insensible.

If such had been the case, I reasoned that it was altogether unlikely that the trivial impression as to President Byxbee had been the only one which I had received in that state. It was far more probable that it had remained over in my mind, on waking from the swoon, merely because it was the latest of a series of impressions received while outside the body. That these impressions were of a kind most strange and startling, seeing that they were those of a disembodied soul exercising faculties more spiritual than those of the body, I could not doubt. The desire to know what they had been grew upon me, till it became a longing which left me no repose. It seemed intolerable that I should have secrets from myself, that my soul should withhold its experiences from my intellect. I would gladly have consented that the acquisitions of half my waking lifetime should be blotted out, if so be in exchange I might be shown the record of what I had seen and known during those hours of which my waking memory showed no trace. None the less for the conviction of its hopelessness, but rather all the more, as the perversity of our human nature will have it, the longing for this forbidden lore grew on me, till the hunger of Eve in the Garden was mine.

Constantly brooding over a desire that I felt to be vain, tantalized by the possession of a clue which only mocked me, my physical condition became at length affected. My health was disturbed and my rest at night was broken. A habit of walking in my sleep, from which I had not suffered since childhood, recurred, and caused me frequent inconvenience. Such had been, in general, my condition for some time, when I awoke one morning with the strangely weary sensation by which my body usually betrayed the secret of the impositions put upon it in sleep, of which otherwise I should often have suspected nothing. In going into the study connected with my chamber, I found a number of freshly written sheets on the desk. Astonished that anyone should have been in my rooms while I slept, I was astounded, on looking more closely, to observe that the handwriting was my own. How much more than astounded I was on reading the matter that had been set down, the reader may judge if he shall peruse it. For these written sheets apparently contained the longed for but despaired of record of those hours when I was absent from the body. They were the lost chapter of my life; or rather, not lost at all, for it had been no part of my waking life, but a stolen chapter — stolen from that sleep-memory on whose mysterious tablets may well be inscribed tales as much more marvellous than this as this is stranger than most stories.

It will be remembered that my last recollection before awaking in my bed, on the morning after the swoon, was of contemplating the coast of Kepler Land with an unusual concentration of attention. As well as I can judge — and that is no better than anyone else — it is with the moment that my bodily powers succumbed and I became unconscious that the narrative which I found on my desk begins.

THE DOCUMENT FOUND ON MY DESK

Even had I not come as straight and swift as the beam of light that made my path, a glance about would have told me to what part of the universe I had fared. No earthly landscape could have been more familiar. I stood on the high coast of Kepler Land where it trends southward. A brisk westerly wind was blowing and the waves of the Ocean of De La Rue were thundering at my feet, while the broad blue waters of Christie Bay stretched away to the southwest. Against the northern horizon, rising out of the ocean like a summer thunder-head, for which at first I mistook it, towered the far distant, snowy summit of Mount Hall.

Even had the configuration of land and sea been less familiar, I should none the less have known that I stood on the planet whose ruddy hue is at once the admiration and puzzle of astronomers. Its explanation I now recognized in the tint of the atmosphere, a colouring comparable to the haze of Indian summer, except that its hue was a faint rose instead of purple. Like the Indian summer haze, it was impalpable, and without impeding the view bathed all objects near and far in a glamour not to be described. As the gaze turned upward, however, the deep blue of space so far overcame the roseate tint that one might fancy he were still on Earth.

As I looked about me I saw many men, women and children. They were in no respect dissimilar, so far as I could see, to the men, women and children of the Earth, save for something almost childlike in the untroubled serenity of their faces, unfurrowed as they were by any trace of care, of fear or of anxiety. This extraordinary youthfulness of aspect made it difficult, indeed, save by careful scrutiny, to distinguish the young from the middle-aged, maturity from advanced years. Time seemed to have no tooth on Mars.

I was gazing about me, admiring this crimson-lighted world, and these people, who appeared to hold happiness by a tenure so much firmer than men's, when I heard the words, "You are welcome", and, turning, saw that I had been accosted by a man with the stature and bearing of middle age, though his countenance, like the other faces which I had noted, wonderfully combined the strength of a man's with the serenity of a child's. I thanked him, and said —

"You do not seem surprised to see me though I certainly am to find myself here."

"Assuredly not", he answered. "I knew, of course, that I was to meet you today. And not only that, but I may say I am already in a sense acquainted with you, through a mutual friend, Professor Edgerly. He was here last month, and I met him at that time. We talked of you and your interest in our planet. I told him I expected you."

"Edgerly!" I exclaimed. "It is strange that he has said nothing of this to me. I meet him every day."

But I was reminded that it was a dream that Edgerly, like

myself, had visited Mars, and on awaking had recalled nothing of his experience, just as I should recall nothing of mine. When will man learn to interrogate the dream soul of the marvels it sees in its wanderings? Then he will no longer need to improve his telescopes to find out the secrets of the universe.

"Do your people visit the Earth in the same manner?" I asked my companion.

"Certainly", he replied; "but there we find no one able to recognize us and converse with us as I am conversing with you, although myself in the waking state. You, as yet, lack the knowledge we possess of the spiritual side of the human nature which we share with you."

"That knowledge must have enabled you to learn much more of the Earth than we know of you", I said.

"Indeed it has", he replied. "From visitors such as you, of whom we entertain a concourse constantly, we have acquired familiarity with your civilization, your history, your manners and even your literature and languages. Have you not noticed that I am talking with you in English, which is certainly not a tongue indigenous to this planet?"

"Among so many wonders I scarcely observed that", I answered.

"For ages", pursued my companion, "we have been waiting for you to improve your telescopes so as to approximate the power of ours, after which communication between the planets would be easily established. The progress which you make is, however, so slow that we expect to wait ages yet."

"Indeed, I fear you will have to", I replied. "Our opticians already talk of having reached the limits of their art."

"Do not imagine that I spoke in any spirit of petulance", my companion resumed. "The slowness of your progress is not so remarkable to us as that you make any at all, burdened as you are by a disability so crushing that if we were in your place I fear we should sit down in utter despair."

"To what disability do you refer?" I asked. "You seem to be men like us."

"And so we are," was the reply, "save in one particular, but there the difference is tremendous. Endowed otherwise like us, you are destitute of the faculty of foresight, without which we should think our other faculties well nigh valueless."

"Foresight!" I repeated. "Certainly you cannot mean that it is given you to know the future?"

"It is given not only to us," was the answer, "but so far as we know, to all other intelligent beings of the universe except yourselves. Our positive knowledge extends only to our system of moons and planets and some of the nearer foreign systems, and it is conceivable that the remoter parts of the universe may harbour other blind races like your own; but it certainly seems unlikely that so strange and lamentable a spectacle should be duplicated. One such illustration of the extraordinary deprivations under which a rational existence may still be possible ought to suffice for the universe."

"But no one can know the future except by inspiration of God", I said.

"All our faculties are by inspiration of God," was the reply, "but there is surely nothing in foresight to cause it to be so regarded more than any other. Think a moment of the physical analogy of the case. Your eyes are placed in the front of your heads. You would deem it an odd mistake if they were placed behind. That would appear to you an arrangement calculated to defeat their purpose. Does it not seem equally rational that the mental vision should range forward, as it does with us, illuminating the path one is to take, rather than backward, as with you, revealing only the course you have already trodden, and therefore have no more concern with? But it is no doubt a merciful provision of Providence that renders you unable to realize the grotesqueness of your predicament, as it appears to us."

"But the future is eternal!" I exclaimed. "How can a finite mind grasp it?"

"Our foreknowledge implies only human faculties", was the reply. "It is limited to our individual careers on this planet. Each of us foresees the course of his own life, but not that of other lives, except so far as they are involved with his."

"That such a power as you describe could be combined with merely human faculties is more than our philosophers have ever dared to dream", I said. "And yet who shall say, after all, that it is not in mercy that God has denied it to us? If it is happiness, as it must be, to foresee one's happiness, it must also be most depressing to foresee one's sorrows, failures, yes, and even one's death. For if you foresee your lives to the end, you must anticipate the hour and manner of your death — is it not so?" "Most assuredly", was the reply. "Living would be a very precarious business were we uninformed of its limit. Your ignorance of the time of your death impresses us as one of the saddest features of your condition." "And by us", I answered, "it is held to be one of the most merciful."

"Foreknowledge of your death would not, indeed, prevent your dying once," continued my companion, "but it would deliver you from the thousand deaths you suffer through uncertainty whether you can safely count on the passing day. It is not the death you die, but these many deaths you do not die, which shadow your existence. Poor blindfolded creatures that you are, cringing at every step in apprehension of the stroke that perhaps is not to fall till old age, never raising a cup to your lips with the knowledge that you will live to quaff it, never sure that you will meet again the friend you part with for an hour, from whose hearts no happiness suffices to banish the chill of an ever-present dread, what idea can you form of the godlike security with which we enjoy our lives and the lives of those we love! You have a saying on Earth, 'Tomorrow belongs to God'; but here tomorrow belongs to us, even as today. To you, for some inscrutable purpose, He sees fit to dole out life moment by moment, with no assurance that each is not to be the last. To us He gives a lifetime at once, fifty, sixty, seventy years — a divine gift, indeed. A life such as yours would, I fear, seem of little value to us; for such a life, however long, is but a moment long, since that is all you can count on."

"And yet," I answered, "though knowledge of the duration of your lives may give you an enviable feeling of confidence while the end is far off, is that not more than offset by the daily growing weight with which the expectation of the end, as it draws near, must press upon your minds?"

"On the contrary," was the response, "death, never an object of fear, as it draws nearer becomes more and more a matter of indifference to the moribund. It is because you live in the past that death is grievous to you. All your knowledge, all your affections, all your interests, are rooted in the past, and on that account, as life lengthens, it strengthens its hold on you, and memory becomes a more precious possession. We, on the contrary, despise the past, and never dwell upon it. Memory with us, far from being the morbid and monstrous growth it is with you, is scarcely more than a rudimentary faculty. We live wholly in the future and the present. What with foretaste and actual taste, our experiences, whether pleasant or painful, are exhausted of interest by the time they are past. The accumulated treasures of memory, which you relinquish so painfully in death, we count no loss at all. Our minds being fed wholly from the future, we think and feel only as we anticipate; and so, as the dying man's future contracts, there is less and less about which he can occupy his thoughts. His interest in life diminishes as the ideas which it suggests grow fewer, till at the last death finds him with his mind a *tabula rasa,* as with you at birth. In a word, his concern with life is reduced to a vanishing point before he is called on to give it up. In dying he leaves nothing behind."

"And the after-death," I asked — "is there no fear of that?"

"Surely", was the reply, "it is not necessary for me to say that a fear which affects only the more ignorant on Earth is not known at all to us, and would be counted blasphemous. Moreover, as I have said, our foresight is limited to our lives on this planet. Any speculation beyond them would be purely conjectural, and our minds are repelled by the slightest taint of uncertainty. To us the conjectural and the unthinkable may be called almost the same."

"But even if you do not fear death for itself," I said, "you have hearts to break. Is there no pain when the ties of love are sundered?"

"Love and death are not foes on our planet", was the reply. "There are no tears by the bedsides of our dying. The same beneficent law which makes it so easy for us to give up life forbids us to mourn the friends we leave, or them to mourn us. With you, it is the intercourse you have had with friends that is the source of your tenderness for them. With us, it is the anticipation of the intercourse we shall enjoy which is the foundation of fondness. As our friends vanish from our future with the approach of their death, the effect on our thoughts and affections is as it would be with you if you forgot them by lapse of time. As our dying friends grow more and more indifferent to us, we, by operation of the same law of our nature, become indifferent to them, till at the last we are scarcely more than kindly and sympathetic watchers about the beds of those who regard us equally without keen emotions. So at last God gently unwinds instead of breaking the bands that bind our hearts together, and makes death as painless to the surviving as to the dying. Relations meant to produce our happiness are not the means also of torturing us, as with you. Love means joy, and that alone, to us, instead of blessing our lives for a while only to desolate them later on, compelling us to pay with a distinct and separate pang for every thrill of tenderness, exacting a tear for every smile."

"There are other partings than those of death. Are these, too, without sorrow for you?" I asked.

"Assuredly", was the reply. "Can you not see that so it must needs be with beings freed by foresight from the disease of memory? All the sorrow of parting, as of dying, comes with you from the backward vision which precludes you from beholding your happiness till it is past. Suppose your life destined to be blest by a happy friendship. If you could know it beforehand, it would be a joyous expectation, brightening the intervening years and cheering you as you traversed desolate periods. But no; not till you meet the one who is to be your friend do you know of him. Nor do you guess even then what he is to be to you, that you may embrace him at first sight. Your meeting is cold and indifferent. It is long before the fire is fairly kindled between you, and then it is already time for parting. Now, indeed, the fire burns well, but henceforth it must consume your heart. Not till they are dead or gone do you fully realize how dear your friends were and how sweet was their companionship. But we — we see our friends afar off coming to meet us, smiling already in our eyes, years before our ways meet. We greet them at first meeting, not coldly, not uncertainly, but with exultant kisses, in an ecstasy of joy. They enter at once into the full possession of hearts long warmed and lighted for them. We meet with that delirium of tenderness with which you part. And when to us at last the time of parting comes, it only means that we are to contribute to each other's happiness no longer. We are not doomed, like you, in parting, to take away with us the delight we brought our friends, leaving the ache of bereavement in its place, so that their last state is worse than their first. Parting here is like meeting with you, calm and unimpassioned. The joys of anticipation and possession are the only food of love with us, and therefore Love always wears a smiling face. With you he feeds on dead joys, past happiness, which are likewise the sustenance of sorrow. No wonder love and sorrow are so much alike on Earth. It is a common saying among us that, were it not for the spectacle of the Earth, the rest of the worlds would be unable to appreciate the goodness of God to them; and who can say that this is not the reason the piteous sight is set before us?"

"You have told me marvellous things", I said, after I had reflected. "It is, indeed, but reasonable that such a race as yours should look down with wondering pity on the Earth. And yet, before I grant so much, I want to ask you one question. There is known in our world a certain sweet madness, under the influence of which we forget all that is untoward in our lot, and would not change it for a god's. So far is this sweet madness regarded by men as a compensation, and more than a compensation, for all their miseries that if you know not love as we know it, if this loss be the price you have paid for your divine foresight, we think ourselves more favoured of God than you. Confess that love, with its reserves, its surprises, its mysteries, its revelations, is necessarily incompatible with a foresight which weighs and measures every experience in advance."

"Of love's surprises we certainly know nothing", was the reply. "It is believed by our philosophers that the slightest surprise would kill beings of our constitution like lightning; though of course this is merely theory, for it is only by the study of Earthly conditions that we are able to form an idea of what surprise is like. Your power to endure the constant buffetings of the unexpected is a matter of supreme amazement to us; nor, according to our ideas, is there any difference between what you call pleasant and painful surprises. You see, then, that we cannot envy you these surprises of love which you find so sweet, for to us they would be fatal. For the rest, there is no form of happiness which foresight is so well calculated to enhance as that of love. Let me explain to you how this befalls. As the growing boy begins to be sensible of the charms of woman, he finds himself, as I dare say it is with you, preferring some type of face and form to others. He dreams oftenest of fair hair or maybe of dark, of blue eyes or brown. As the years go on, his fancy, brooding over what seems to it the best and loveliest of every type, is constantly adding to this dream-face, this shadowy form, traits and lineaments, hues and contours, till at last the picture is complete, and he becomes aware that on his heart thus subtly has been depicted the likeness of the maiden destined for his arms.

"It may be years before he is to see her, but now begins with him one of the sweetest offices of love, one to you unknown. Youth on Earth is a stormy period of passion, chafing in restraint or rioting in excess. But the very passion whose awaking makes this time so critical with you is here a reforming and educating influence, to whose gentle and potent sway we gladly confide our children. The temptations which lead your young men astray have no hold on a youth of our happy planet. He hoards the treasures of his heart for its coming mistress. Of her alone he thinks, and to her all his vows are made. The thought of license would be treason to his sovereign lady, whose right to all the revenues of his being he joyfully owns. To rob her, to abate her high prerogatives, would be to impoverish, to insult himself; for she is to be his, and her honour, her glory are his own. Through all this time that he dreams of her by night and day, the exquisite reward of his devotion is the knowledge that she is aware of him as he of her, and that in the inmost shrine of a maiden heart his image is set up to receive the incense of a tenderness that needs not to restrain itself through fear of possible cross or separation.

"In due time their converging lives come together. The lovers meet, gaze a moment into each other's eyes, then throw themselves each on the other's breast. The maiden has all the charms that ever stirred the blood of an Earthly lover, but there is another glamour over her which the eyes of Earthly lovers are shut to — the glamour of the future. In the blushing girl her lover sees the fond and faithful wife, in the blithe maiden the patient, pain-consecrated mother. On the virgin's breast he beholds his children. He is prescient, even as his lips take the first-fruits of hers, of the future years during which she is to be his companion, his ever-present solace, his chief portion of God's goodness. We have read some of your romances describing love as you know it on Earth, and I must confess, my friend, we find them very dull. "I hope", he added, as I did not at once speak, "that I shall not offend you by saying we find them also objectionable. Your literature possesses in general an interest for us in the picture it presents of the curiously inverted life which the lack of foresight compels you to lead. It is a study especially prized for the development of the imagination, on account of the difficulty of conceiving conditions so opposed to those of intelligent beings in general. But our women do not read your romances. The notion that a man or woman should ever conceive the idea of marrying a person other than the one whose husband or wife he or she is destined to be is profoundly shocking to our habits of thought. No doubt you will say that such instances are rare among you, but if your novels are faithful pictures of your life, they are at least not unknown. That these situations are inevitable under the conditions of earthly life we are well aware, and judge you accordingly; but it is needless that the minds of our maidens should be pained by the knowledge that there anywhere exists a world where such travesties upon the sacredness of marriage are possible.

"There is, however, another reason why we discourage the use of your books by our young people, and that is the profound effect of sadness, to a race accustomed to view all things in the morning-glow of the future, of a literature written in the past tense and relating exclusively to things that are ended."

"And how do you write of things that are past except in the past tense?" I asked.

"We write of the past when it is still the future, and of course in the future tense", was the reply. "If our historians were to wait till after the events to describe them, not alone would nobody care to read about things already done, but the histories themselves would probably be inaccurate; for memory, as I have said, is a very slightly developed faculty with us, and quite too indistinct to be trustworthy. Should the Earth ever establish communication with us, you will find our histories of interest; for our planet, being smaller, cooled and was peopled ages before yours, and our astronomical records contain minute accounts of the Earth from the time it was a fluid mass. Your geologists and biologists may yet find a mine of information here."

In the course of our further conversation it came out that, as a consequence of foresight, some of the commonest emotions of human nature are unknown on Mars. They for whom the future has no mystery can, of course, know neither hope nor fear. Moreover, everyone being assured what he shall attain to and what not, there can be no such thing as rivalship, or emulation, or any sort of competition in any respect; and therefore all the brood of heart-burnings and hatreds, engendered on Earth by the strife of man with man, is unknown to the people of Mars, save from the study of our planet. When I asked if there were not, after all, a lack of spontaneity, of sense of freedom, in leading lives fixed in all details beforehand, I was reminded that there was no difference in that respect between the lives of the people of Earth and Mars, both alike being according to God's will in every particular. We knew that will only after the event, they before — that was all. For the rest, God moved them through their wills as He did us, so that they had no more sense of compulsion in what they did than we on Earth have in carrying out an anticipated line of action, in cases where our anticipations chance to be correct. Of the absorbing interest which the study of the plan of their future lives possessed for the people of Mars, my companion spoke eloquently. It was, he said, like the fascination to a mathematician of a most elaborate and exquisite demonstration, a perfect algebraical equation, with the glowing realities of life in place of figures and symbols.

When I asked if it never occurred to them to wish their futures different, he replied that such a question could only have been asked by one from the Earth. No one could have foresight, or clearly believe that God had it, without realizing that the future is as incapable of being changed as the past. And not only this, but to foresee events was to foresee their logical necessity so clearly that to desire them different was as impossible as seriously to wish that two and two made five instead of four. No person could ever thoughtfully wish anything different, for so closely are all things, the small with the great, woven together by God that to draw out the smallest thread would unravel creation through all eternity.

While we had talked the afternoon had waned, and the sun had sunk below the horizon, the roseate atmosphere of the planet imparting a splendour to the cloud colouring, and a glory to the land and seascape, never paralleled by an Earthly sunset. Already the familiar constellations appearing in the sky reminded me how near, after all, I was to the Earth, for with the unassisted eye I could not detect the slightest variation in their position. Nevertheless, there was one wholly novel feature in the heavens, for many of the host of asteroids which circle in the zone between Mars and Jupiter were vividly visible to the naked eye. But the spectacle that chiefly held my gaze was the Earth, swimming low on the verge of the horizon. Its disc, twice as large as that of any star or planet as seen from the Earth, flashed with a brilliancy like that of Venus.

"It is, indeed, a lovely sight," said my companion, "although to me always a melancholy one, from the contrast suggested between the radiance of the orb and the benighted condition of its inhabitants. We call it 'The Blind Man's World'." As he spoke he turned towards a curious structure which stood near us, though I had not before particularly observed it.

"What is that?" I asked.

"It is one of our telescopes", he replied. "I am going to let you take a look, if you choose, at your home, and test for yourself the powers of which I have boasted", and having adjusted the instrument to his satisfaction, he showed me where to apply my eye to what answered to the eyepiece.

I could not repress an exclamation of amazement, for truly he had exaggerated nothing. The little college town which was my home lay spread out before me, seemingly almost as near as when I looked down upon it from my observatory windows. It was early morning, and the village was waking up. The milkmen were going their rounds, and workmen, with their dinner pails, were hurrying along the streets. The early train was just leaving the railroad station. I could see the puffs from the smoke-stack, and the jets from the cylinders. It was strange not to hear the hissing of the steam, so near I seemed. There were the college buildings on the hill, the long rows of windows flashing back the level sunbeams. I could tell the time by the college clock. It struck me that there was unusual bustle around the buildings, considering the earliness of the hour. A crowd of men stood about the door of the observatory, and many others were hurrying across the campus in that direction. Among them I recognized President Byxbee, accompanied by the college janitor. As I gazed they reached the observatory, and, passing through the group about the door, entered the building. The president was evidently going up to my quarters. At this it flashed over me quite suddenly that all this bustle was on my account. I recalled how it was that I came to be on Mars, and in what condition I had left affairs in the observatory. It was high time I were back there to look after myself.

Here abruptly ended the extraordinary document which I found that morning on my desk. That it is the authentic record of the conditions of life in another world which it purports to be I do not expect the reader to believe. He will no doubt explain it as another of the curious freaks of somnambulism set down in the books. Probably it was merely that, possibly it was something more. I do not pretend to decide the question. I have told all the facts of the case, and have no better means for forming an opinion than the reader. Nor do I know, even if I fully believed it the true account it seems to be, that it would have affected my imagination much more strongly than it has. That story of another world has, in a word, put me out of joint with ours. The readiness with which my mind has adapted itself to the Martial point of view concerning the Earth has been a singular experience. The lack of foresight among the human faculties, a lack I had scarcely thought of before, now impresses me, ever more deeply, as a fact out of harmony with the rest of our nature, belying its promise — a moral mutilation, a deprivation arbitrary and unaccountable. The spectacle of a race doomed to walk backward, beholding only what has gone by, assured only of what is past and dead, comes over me from time to time with a sadly fantastical effect which I cannot describe. I dream of a world where love always wears a smile, where the partings are as tearless as our meetings, and death is king no more. I have a fancy, which I like to cherish, that the people of that happy sphere, fancied though it may be, represent the ideal and normal type of our race, as perhaps it once was, as perhaps it may yet be again.

TO WHOM THIS MAY COME

It is now about a year since I took passage at Calcutta in the ship Adelaide for New York. We had baffling weather till New Amsterdam Island was sighted, where we took a new point of departure. Three days later a terrible gale struck us. Four days we flew before it, whither, no one knew, for neither sun, moon nor stars were at any time visible, and we could take no observation. Towards midnight of the fourth day, the glare of lightning revealed the Adelaide in a hopeless position, close in upon a low-lying shore and driving straight towards it. All around and astern far out to sea was such a maze of rocks and shoals that it was a miracle we had come so far. Presently the ship struck and almost instantly went to pieces, so great was the violence of the sea. I gave myself up for lost and was indeed already past the worst of drowning, when I was recalled to consciousness by being thrown with a tremendous shock upon the beach. I had just strength enough to drag myself above the reach of the waves, and then I fell down and knew no more.

When I awoke, the storm was over. The sun, already halfway up the sky, had dried my clothing and renewed the vigour of my bruised and aching limbs. On sea or shore I saw no vestige of my ship or my companions, of whom I appeared the sole survivor. I was not, however, alone. A group of persons, apparently the inhabitants of the country, stood near, observing me with looks of friendliness which at once freed me from apprehension as to my treatment at their hands. They were a white and handsome people, evidently of a high order of civilization, though I recognized in them the traits of no race with which I was familiar.

Seeing that it was evidently their idea of etiquette to leave it to strangers to open conversation, I addressed them in English, but failed to elicit any response beyond deprecating smiles. I then accosted them successively in the French, German, Italian, Spanish, Dutch and Portuguese tongues, but with no better results. I began to be very much puzzled as to what could possibly be the nationality of a white and evidently civilized race to which no one of the tongues of the great seafaring nations was intelligible. The oddest thing of all was the unbroken silence with which they contemplated my efforts to open communication with them. It was as if they were agreed not to give me a clue to their language by even a whisper; for while they regarded one another with looks of smiling intelligence, they did not once open their lips. But if this behaviour suggested that they were amusing themselves at my expense, that presumption was negatived by the unmistakable friendliness and sympathy which their whole bearing expressed.

A most extraordinary conjecture occurred to me. Could it be that these strange people were dumb? Such a freak of nature as an entire race thus afflicted had never indeed been heard of, but who could say what wonders the unexplored vasts of the great southern ocean might thus far have hid from human ken? Now, among the scraps of useless information which lumbered my mind, was an acquaintance with the deaf-and-dumb alphabet, and forthwith I began to spell out with my fingers some of the phrases I had already uttered to so little effect. My resort to the sign language overcame the last remnant of gravity in the already profusely smiling group. The small boys now rolled on the ground in convulsions of mirth, while the grave and reverend seniors, who had hitherto kept them in check, were fain momentarily to avert their faces, and I could see their bodies shaking with laughter. The greatest clown in the world never received a more flattering tribute to his powers to amuse than had been called forth by mine to make myself understood. Naturally, however, I was not flattered, but on the contrary entirely discomfited. Angry I could not well be, for the deprecating manner in which all, excepting of course the boys, yielded to their perception of the ridiculous, and the distress they showed at their failure in self-control, made me seem the aggressor. It was as if they were very sorry for me and ready to put themselves wholly at my service if I would only refrain from reducing them to a state of disability by being so exquisitely absurd. Certainly this evidently amiable race had a very embarrassing way of receiving strangers.

Just at this moment, when my bewilderment was fast verging on exasperation, relief came. The circle opened, and a little elderly man, who had evidently come in haste, confronted me and, bowing very politely, addressed me in English. His voice was the most pitiable abortion of a voice I had ever heard. While having all the defects in articulation of a child's who is just beginning to talk, it was not even a child's in strength of tone, being in fact a mere alternation of squeaks and whispers inaudible a rod away. With some difficulty I was, however, able to follow him pretty nearly.

"As the official interpreter," he said, "I extend you a cordial welcome to these islands. I was sent for as soon as you were discovered, but being at some distance, I was unable to arrive until this moment. I regret this, as my presence would have saved you embarrassment. My countrymen desire me to intercede with you to pardon the wholly involuntary and uncontrollable mirth provoked by your attempts to communicate with them. You see, they understood you perfectly well, but could not answer you."

"Merciful heavens!" I exclaimed, horrified to find my surmise correct, "can it be that they are all thus afflicted? Is it possible that you are the only man among them who has the power of speech?"

Again it appeared that, quite unintentionally, I had said something excruciatingly funny, for at my speech there arose a sound of gentle laughter from the group, now augmented to quite an assemblage, which drowned the plashing of the waves on the beach at our feet. Even the interpreter smiled.

"Do they think it so amusing to be dumb?" I asked.

"They find it very amusing", replied the interpreter, "that their inability to speak should be regarded by anyone as an affliction, for it is by the voluntary disuse of the organs of articulation that they have lost the power of speech and, as a consequence, the ability even to understand speech."

"But", said I, somewhat puzzled by this statement, "didn't you just tell me that they understood me, though they could not reply, and are they not laughing now at what I just said?"

"It is you they understood, not your words", answered the interpreter. "Our speech now is gibberish to them, as unintelligible in itself as the growling of animals; but they know what we are saying, because they know our thoughts. You must know that these are the islands of the mind-readers."

Such were the circumstances of my introduction to this extraordinary people. The official interpreter being charged by virtue of his office with the first entertainment of shipwrecked members of the talking nations, I became his guest and passed a number of days under his roof before going out to any considerable extent among the people. My first impression had been the somewhat oppressive one that the power to read the thoughts of others could be possessed only by beings of a superior order to man. It was the first effort of the interpreter to disabuse me of this notion. It appeared from his account that the experience of the mind-readers was a case simply of a slight acceleration, from special causes, of the course of universal human evolution, which in time was destined to lead to the disuse of speech and the substitution of direct mental vision on the part of all races. This rapid evolution of these islanders was accounted for by their peculiar origin and circumstances.

Some three centuries before Christ, one of the Parthian kings of Persia, of the dynasty of the Arsacidae, undertook a persecution of the soothsayers and magicians in his realms. These people were credited with supernatural powers by popular prejudice, but in fact were merely persons of special gifts in the way of hypnotizing, mind-reading, thought transference and such arts, which they exercised for their own gain.

Too much in awe of the soothsayers to do them outright violence, the king resolved to banish them, and to this end put them, with their families, on ships and sent them to Ceylon. When, however, the fleet was in the neighbourhood of that island, a great storm scattered it, and one of the ships, after being driven for many days before the tempest, was wrecked upon one of an archipelago of uninhabited islands far to the south, where the survivors settled. Naturally, the posterity of the parents possessed of such peculiar gifts had developed extraordinary psychical powers.

Having set before them the end of evolving a new and advanced order of humanity, they had aided the development of these powers by a rigid system of stirpiculture. The result was that, after a few centuries, mind-reading became so general that language fell into disuse as a means of communicating ideas. For many generations the power of speech still remained voluntary, but gradually the vocal organs had become atrophied, and for several hundred years the power of articulation had been wholly lost. Infants for a few months after birth did, indeed, still emit inarticulate cries, but at an age when in less advanced races these cries began to be articulate, the children of the mind-readers developed the power of direct vision and ceased to attempt to use the voice.

The fact that the existence of the mind-readers had never been found out by the rest of the world was explained by two considerations. In the first place, the group of islands was small and occupied a corner of the Indian Ocean quite out of the ordinary track of ships. In the second place, the approach to the islands was rendered so desperately perilous by terrible currents and the maze of outlying rocks and shoals that it was next to impossible for any ship to touch their shores save as a wreck. No ship at least had ever done so in the two thousand years since the mind-readers' own arrival, and the Adelaide had made the one hundred and twenty-third such wreck.

Apart from motives of humanity, the mind-readers made strenuous efforts to rescue shipwrecked persons, for from them alone, through the interpreters, could they obtain information of the outside world. Little enough this proved when, as often happened, the sole survivor of the shipwreck was some ignorant sailor, who had no news to communicate beyond the latest varieties of forecastle blasphemy. My hosts gratefully assured me that, as a person of some little education, they considered me a veritable godsend. No less a task was mine than to relate to them the history of the world for the past two centuries, and often did I wish, for their sakes, that I had made a more exact study of it.

It is solely for the purpose of communicating with shipwrecked strangers of the talking nations that the office of the interpreters exists. When, as from time to time happens, a child is born with some powers of articulation, he is set apart, and trained to talk in the interpreters' college. Of course, the partial atrophy of the vocal organs, from which even the best interpreters suffer, renders many of the sounds of language impossible for them. None, for instance, can pronounce *v, f,* or *s*; and as to the sound represented by *th,* it is five generations since the last interpreter lived who could utter it. But for the occasional intermarriage of shipwrecked strangers with the islanders, it is probable that the supply of interpreters would have long ere this quite failed.

I imagine that the very unpleasant sensations which followed the realization that I was among people who, while inscrutable to me, knew my every thought, were very much what anyone would have experienced in the same case. They were very comparable to the panic which accidental nudity causes a person among races whose custom it is to conceal the figure with drapery. I wanted to run away and hide myself. If I analysed my feeling, it did not seem to arise so much from the consciousness of any particularly heinous secrets, as from the knowledge of a swarm of fatuous, ill-natured and unseemly thoughts and half thoughts concerning those around me, and concerning myself, which it was insufferable that any person should peruse in however benevolent a spirit. But while my chagrin and distress on this account were at first intense, they were also very short-lived, for almost immediately I discovered that the very knowledge that my mind was overlooked by others operated to check thoughts that might be painful to them, and that, too, without more effort of the will than a kindly person exerts to check the utterance of disagreeable remarks. As a very few lessons in the elements of courtesy cures a decent person of inconsiderate speaking, so a brief experience among the mind-readers went far in my case to check inconsiderate thinking. It must not be supposed, however, that courtesy among the mind-readers prevents them from thinking pointedly and freely concerning one another upon serious occasions, any more than the finest courtesy among the talking races restrains them from speaking to one another with entire plainness when it is desirable to do so. Indeed, among the mind-readers, politeness never can extend to the point of insincerity, as among talking nations, seeing that it is always one another's real and inmost thought that they read. I may fitly mention here, though it was not till later that I fully understood why it must necessarily be so, that one need feel far less chagrin at the complete revelation of his weaknesses to a mind-reader than at the slightest betrayal of them to one of another race. For the very reason that the mind-reader reads all your thoughts, particular thoughts are judged with reference to the general tenor of thought. Your characteristic and habitual frame of mind is what he takes account of. No one need fear being misjudged by a mind-reader on account of sentiments or emotions which are not representative of the real character or general attitude. Justice may, indeed, be said to be a necessary consequence of mind-reading.

As regards the interpreter himself, the instinct of courtesy was not long needed to check wanton or offensive thoughts. In all my life before, I had been very slow to form friendships, but before I had been three days in the company of this stranger of a strange race, I had become enthusiastically devoted to him. It was impossible not to be. The peculiar joy of friendship is the sense of being understood by our friend as we are not by others, and yet of being loved in spite of the understanding. Now here was one whose every word testified to a knowledge of my secret thoughts and motives which the oldest and nearest of my former friends had never, and could never, have approximated. Had such a knowledge bred in him contempt of me, I should neither have blamed him nor been at all surprised. Judge, then, whether the cordial friendliness which he showed was likely to leave me indifferent.

Imagine my incredulity when he informed me that our friendship was not based upon more than ordinary mutual suitability of temperaments. The faculty of mind-reading, he explained, brought minds so close together, and so heightened sympathy, that the lowest order of friendship between mind-readers implied a mutual delight such as only rare friends enjoyed among other races. He assured me that later on, when I came to know others of his race, I should find, by the far greater intensity of sympathy and affection I should conceive for some of them, how true this saying was.

It may be enquired how, on beginning to mingle with the mind-readers in general, I managed to communicate with them, seeing that, while they could read my thoughts, they could not, like the interpreter, respond to them by speech. I must here explain that, while these people have no use for a spoken language, a written language is needful for purposes of record. They consequently all know how to write. Do they, then, write Persian? Luckily for me, no. It appears that, for a long period after mind-reading was fully developed, not only was spoken language disused, but also written, no records whatever having been kept during this period. The delight of the people in the newly found power of direct mind-to-mind vision, whereby pictures of the total mental state were communicated, instead of the imperfect descriptions of single thoughts which words at best could give, induced an invincible distaste for the laborious impotence of language.

When, however, the first intellectual intoxication had, after several generations, somewhat sobered down, it was recognized that records of the past were desirable, and that the despised medium of words was needful to preserve it. Persian had meanwhile been wholly forgotten. In order to avoid the prodigious task of inventing a complete new language, the institution of the interpreters was now set up, with the idea of acquiring through them a knowledge of some of the languages of the outside world from the mariners wrecked on the islands.

Owing to the fact that most of the castaway ships were English, a better knowledge of that tongue was acquired than of any other, and it was adopted as the written language of the people. As a rule, my acquaintances wrote slowly and laboriously, and yet the fact that they knew exactly what was in my mind rendered their responses so apt that, in my conversations with the slowest speller of them all, the interchange of thought was as rapid and incomparably more accurate and satisfactory than the fastest talkers attain to.

It was but a very short time after I had begun to extend my acquaintance among the mind-readers before I discovered how truly the interpreter had told me that I should find others to whom, on account of greater natural congeniality, I should become more strongly attached than I had been to him. This was in no wise, however, because I loved him less, but them more. I would fain write particularly of some of these beloved friends, comrades of my heart, from whom I first learnt the undreamt of possibilities of human friendship and how ravishing the satisfactions of sympathy may be. Who, among those who may read this, has not known that sense of a gulf fixed between soul and soul which mocks love! Who has not felt that loneliness which oppresses the heart that loves it best! Think no longer that this gulf is eternally fixed, or is any necessity of human nature. It has no existence for the race of our fellow-men which I describe, and by that fact we may be assured that eventually it will be bridged also for us. Like the touch of shoulder to shoulder, like the clasping of hands, is the contact of their minds and their sensation of sympathy.

I say that I would fain speak more particularly of some of my friends, but waning strength forbids, and moreover, now that I think of it, another consideration would render any comparison of their characters rather confusing than instructive to a reader. This is the fact that, in common with the rest of the mind-readers, they had no names. Every one had, indeed, an arbitrary sign for his designation in records, but it has no sound value. A register of these names is kept so they can at any time be ascertained, but it is very common to meet persons who have forgotten titles which are used solely for biographical and official purposes. For social intercourse names are of course superfluous, for these people accost one another merely by a mental act of attention and refer to third persons by transferring their mental pictures — something as dumb persons might by means of photographs. Something so, I say, for in the pictures of one another's personalities which the mind-readers conceive, the physical aspect, as might be expected with people who directly contemplate each other's minds and hearts, is a subordinate element.

I have already told how my first qualms of morbid self-consciousness at knowing that my mind was an open book to all around me disappeared as I learnt that the very completeness of the disclosure of my thoughts and motives was a guarantee that I would be judged with a fairness and a sympathy such as even self-judgement cannot pretend to, affected as that is by so many subtle reactions. The assurance of being so judged by everyone might well seem an inestimable privilege to one accustomed to a world in which not even the tenderest love is any pledge of comprehension, and yet I soon discovered that open-mindedness had a still greater profit than this. How shall I describe the delightful exhilaration of moral health and cleanness, the breezy oxygenated mental condition, which resulted from the consciousness that I had absolutely nothing concealed! Truly I may say that I enjoyed myself. I think surely that no one needs to have had my marvellous experience to sympathize with this portion of it. Are we not all ready to agree that this having a curtained chamber where we may go to grovel, out of the sight of our fellows, troubled only by a vague apprehension that God may look over the top, is the most demoralizing incident in the human condition? It is the existence within the soul of this secure refuge of lies which has always been the despair of the saint and the exultation of the knave. It is the foul cellar which taints the whole house above, be it never so fine.

What stronger testimony could there be to the instinctive consciousness that concealment is debauching and openness our only cure, than the world-old conviction of the virtue of confession for the soul, and that the uttermost exposing of one's worst and foulest is the first step towards moral health? The wickedest man, if he could but somehow attain to writhe himself inside out as to his soul, so that its full sickness could be seen, would feel ready for a new life. Nevertheless, owing to the utter impotence of the words to convey mental conditions in their totality, or to give other than mere distortions of them, confession is, we must needs admit, but a mockery of that longing for self-revelation to which it testifies. But think what health and soundness there must be for souls among a people who see in every face a conscience which, unlike their own, they cannot sophisticate, who confess one another with a glance and shrive with a smile! Ah, friends, let me now predict, though ages may elapse before the slow event shall justify me, that in no way will the mutual vision of minds, when at last it shall be perfected, so enhance the blessedness of mankind as by rending the veil of self and leaving no spot of darkness in the mind for lies to hide in. Then shall the soul no longer be a coal smoking among ashes, but a star in a crystal sphere.

From what I have said of the delights which friendship among the mind-readers derives from the perfection of the mental rapport, it may be imagined how intoxicating must be the experience when one of the friends is a woman, and the subtle attractions and correspondences of sex touch with passion the intellectual sympathy. With my first venturing into society I had begun, to their extreme amusement, to fall in love with the women right and left. In the perfect frankness which is the condition of all intercourse among this people, these adorable women told me that what I felt was only friendship, which was a very good thing, but wholly different from love, as I should well know if I were beloved. It was difficult to believe that the melting emotions which I had experienced in their company were the result merely of the friendly and kindly attitude of their minds towards mine; but when I found that I was affected in the same way by every gracious woman I met, I had to make up my mind that they must be right about it, and that I should have to adapt myself to a world in which, friendship being a passion, love must needs be nothing less than rapture.

The homely proverb, "Every Jack has his Jill", may, I suppose, be taken to mean that for all men there are certain women expressly suited by mental and moral as well as by physical constitution. It is a thought painful, rather than cheering, that this may be the truth, so altogether do the chances preponderate against the ability of these elect ones to recognize each other even if they meet, seeing that speech is so inadequate and so misleading a medium of self-revelation. But among the mind-readers the search for one's ideal mate is a quest reasonably sure of being crowned with success, and no one dreams of wedding unless it be; for so to do, they consider, would be to throw away the choicest blessing of life, and not alone to wrong themselves and their unfound mates, but likewise those whom they themselves and those undiscovered mates might wed. Therefore, passionate pilgrims, they go from isle to isle till they find each other, and, as the population of the islands is but small, the pilgrimage is not often long.

When I met her first we were in company, and I was struck by the sudden stir and the looks of touched and smiling interest with which all around turned and regarded us, the women with moistened eyes. They had read her thought when she saw me, but this I did not know, neither what was the custom in these matters till afterward. But I knew, from the moment she first fixed her eyes on me and I felt her mind brooding upon mine, how truly I had been told by those other women that the feeling with which they had inspired me was not love.

With people who become acquainted at a glance, and old friends in an hour, wooing is naturally not a long process. Indeed, it may be said that between lovers among mind-readers there is no wooing, but merely recognition. The day after we met she became mine.

Perhaps I cannot better illustrate how subordinate the merely physical element is in the impression which mind-readers form of their friends than by mentioning an incident that occurred some months after our union. This was my discovery, wholly by accident, that my love, in whose society I had almost constantly been, had not the least idea what was the colour of my eyes or whether my hair and complexion were light or dark. Of course, as soon as I asked her the question, she read the answer in my mind, but she admitted that she had previously had no distinct impression on those points. On the other hand, if in the blackest midnight I should come to her, she would not need to ask who the comer was. It is by the mind, not the eye, that these people know one another. It is really only in their relations to soulless and inanimate things that they need eyes at all.

It must not be supposed that their disregard of one another's bodily aspect grows out of any ascetic sentiment. It is merely a necessary consequence of their power of directly apprehending mind that, whenever mind is closely associated with matter, the latter is comparatively neglected on account of the greater interest of the former, suffering as lesser things always do when placed in immediate contrast with greater. Art is with them confined to the inanimate, the human form having, for the reason mentioned, ceased to inspire the artist. It will be naturally and quite correctly inferred that among such a race physical beauty is not the important factor in human fortune and felicity that it elsewhere is. The absolute openness of their minds and hearts to one another makes their happiness far more dependent on the moral and mental qualities of their companions than upon their physical. A genial temperament, a wide-grasping, godlike intellect, a poet soul, are incomparably more fascinating to them than the most dazzling combination conceivable of mere bodily graces.

A woman of mind and heart has no more need of beauty to win love in these islands than a beauty elsewhere of mind or heart. I should mention here, perhaps, that this race, which makes so little account of physical beauty, is itself a singularly handsome one. This is owing doubtless in part to the absolute compatibility of temperaments in all the marriages, and partly also to the reaction upon the body of a state of ideal mental and moral health and placidity.

Not being myself a mind-reader, the fact that my love was rarely beautiful in form and face had doubtless no little part in attracting my devotion. This, of course, she knew, as she knew all my thoughts and, knowing my limitations, tolerated and forgave the element of sensuousness in my passion. But if it must have seemed to her so little worthy in comparison with the high spiritual communion which her race know as love, to me it became, by virtue of her almost superhuman relation to me, an ecstasy more ravishing surely than any lover of my race tasted before. The ache at the heart of the intensest love is the impotence of words to make it perfectly understood to its object. But my passion was without this pang, for my heart was absolutely open to her I loved. Lovers may imagine, but I cannot describe, the ecstatic thrill of communion into which this consciousness transformed every tender emotion. As I considered what mutual love must be where both parties are mind-readers, I realized the high communion which my sweet companion had sacrificed for me. She might indeed comprehend her lover and his love for her, but the higher satisfaction of knowing that she was comprehended by him and her love understood, she had foregone. For that I should ever attain the power of mind-reading was out of the question, the faculty never having been developed in a single lifetime.

Why my inability should move my dear companion to such depths of pity I was not able fully to understand until I learnt that mind-reading is chiefly held desirable, not for the knowledge of others which it gives its possessors, but for the self-knowledge which is its reflex effect. Of all they see in the minds of others, that which concerns them most is the reflection of themselves, the photographs of their own characters. The most obvious consequence of the self-knowledge thus forced upon them is to render them alike incapable of self-conceit or self-depreciation. Everyone must needs always think of himself as he is, being no more able to do otherwise than is a man in a hall of mirrors to cherish delusions as to his personal appearance.

But self-knowledge means to the mind-readers much more than this — nothing less, indeed, than a shifting of the sense of identity. When a man sees himself in a mirror, he is compelled to distinguish between the bodily self he sees and his real self, which is within and unseen. When in turn the mind-reader comes to see the mental and moral self reflected in other minds as in mirrors, the same thing happens. He is compelled to distinguish between this mental and moral self which has been made objective to him, and can be contemplated by him as impartially as if it were another's, from the inner ego which still remains subjective, unseen and indefinable. In this inner ego the mind-readers recognize the essential identity and being, the noumenal self, the core of the soul and the true hiding of its eternal life, to which the mind as well as the body is but the garment of a day.

The effect of such a philosophy as this — which, indeed, with the mind-readers is rather an instinctive consciousness than a philosophy — must obviously be to impart a sense of wonderful superiority to the vicissitudes of this earthly state and a singular serenity in the midst of the haps and mishaps which threaten or befall the personality. They did indeed appear to me, as I never dreamt men could attain to be, lords of themselves.

It was because I might not hope to attain this enfranchisement from the false ego of the apparent self, without which life seemed to her race scarcely worth living, that my love so pitied me.

But I must hasten on, leaving a thousand things unsaid, to relate the lamentable catastrophe to which it is owing that, instead of being still a resident of those blessed islands, in the full enjoyment of that intimate and ravishing companionship which by contrast would forever dim the pleasures of all other human society, I recall the bright picture as a memory under other skies.

Among a people who are compelled by the very constitution of their minds to put themselves in the places of others, the sympathy which is the inevitable consequence of perfect comprehension renders envy, hatred and uncharitableness impossible. But of course there are people less genially constituted than others, and these are necessarily the objects of a certain distaste on the part of associates. Now, owing to the unhindered impact of minds upon one another, the anguish of persons so regarded, despite the tenderest consideration of those about them, is so great that they beg the grace of exile that, being out of the way, people may think less frequently upon them. There are numerous small islets, scarcely more than rocks, lying to the north of the archipelago, and on these the unfortunates are permitted to live. Only one lives on each islet, as they cannot endure each other even as well as the more happily constituted can endure them. From time to time supplies of food are taken to them and, of course, any time they wish to take the risk, they are permitted to return to society.

Now, as I have said, the fact which, even more than their out-of-the-way location, makes the islands of the mind-readers unapproachable is the violence with which the great antarctic current, owing probably to some configuration of the ocean bed, together with the innumerable rocks and shoals, flows through and about the archipelago.

Ships making the islands from the southward are caught by this current and drawn among the rocks, to their almost certain destruction, while, owing to the violence with which the current sets to the north, it is not possible to approach at all from that direction, or at least it has never been accomplished. Indeed, so powerful are the currents that even the boats which cross the narrow straits between the main islands and the islets of the unfortunate, to carry the latter their supplies, are ferried over by cables, not trusting to oar or sail.

The brother of my love had charge of one of the boats engaged in this transportation, and, being desirous of visiting the islets, I accepted an invitation to accompany him on one of his trips. I know nothing of how the accident happened, but in the fiercest part of the current of one of the straits we parted from the cable and were swept out to sea. There was no question of stemming the boiling current, our utmost endeavours barely sufficing to avoid being dashed to pieces on the rocks. From the first, there was no hope of our winning back to the land, and so swiftly did we drift that by noon — the accident having befallen in the morning — the islands, which are low-lying, had sunk beneath the southwestern horizon.

Among these mind-readers, distance is not an insuperable obstacle to the transfer of thought. My companion was in communication with our friends, and from time to time conveyed to me messages of anguish from my dear love, for, being well aware of the nature of the currents and the unapproachableness of the islands, those we had left behind, as well as we ourselves, knew well we should see each other's faces no more. For five days we continued to drift to the northwest, in no danger of starvation owing to our lading of provisions, but constrained to unintermitting watch and ward by the roughness of the weather. On the fifth day my companion died from exposure and exhaustion. He died very quietly — indeed, with great appearance of relief. The life of the mind-readers while yet they are in the body is so largely spiritual that the idea of an existence wholly so, which seems vague and chill to us, suggests to them a state only slightly more refined than they already know on earth.

After that I suppose I must have fallen into an unconscious state, from which I roused to find myself on an American ship bound for New York, surrounded by people whose only means of communicating with one another is to keep up, while together, a constant clatter of hissing, guttural and explosive noises, eked out by all manner of facial contortions and bodily gestures. I frequently find myself staring open-mouthed at those who address me, too much struck by their grotesque appearance to bethink myself of replying.

I find that I shall not live out the voyage, and I do not care to. From my experience of the people on the ship, I can judge how I should fare on land amid the stunning babel of a nation of talkers. And my friends, God bless them! how lonely I should feel in their very presence! Nay, what satisfaction or consolation, what but bitter mockery, could I ever more find in such human sympathy and companionship as suffice others and once sufficed me — I who have seen and known what I have seen and known! Ah, yes, doubtless it is far better I should die, but the knowledge of the things that I have seen I feel should not perish with me. For hope's sake, men should not miss the glimpse of the higher, sun-bathed reaches of the upward path they plod. So thinking, I have written out some account of my wonderful experience, though briefer far, by reason of my weakness, than fits the greatness of the matter. The captain seems an honest well-meaning man, and to him I shall confide the narrative, charging him, on touching shore, to see it safely in the hands of someone who will bring it to the world's ear.

The Nationalist, 1889

A REPUBLIC OF THE GOLDEN RULE

When in the course of the evening the ladies retired, leaving Dr. Leete and myself alone, he sounded me as to my disposition for sleep, saying that if I felt like it my bed was ready for me; but if I was inclined to wakefulness nothing would please him better than to bear me company. "I am a late bird myself," he said, "and, without suspicion of flattery, I may say that a companion more interesting than yourself could scarcely be imagined. It is decidedly not often that one has a chance to converse with a man of the nineteenth century."

Now I had been looking forward all evening with some dread to the time when I should be alone on retiring for the night. Surrounded by these most friendly strangers, stimulated and supported by their sympathetic interest, I had been able to keep my mental balance. Even then, however, in pauses of the conversation I had had glimpses, vivid as lightning flashes, of the horror of strangeness that was waiting to be faced when I could no longer command diversion. I knew I could not sleep that night, and as for lying awake and thinking, it argues no cowardice, I am sure, to confess that I was afraid of it. When, in reply to my host's question, I frankly told him this, he replied that it would be strange if I did not feel just so, but that I need have no anxiety about sleeping; whenever I wanted to go to bed, he would give me a dose which would ensure me a sound night's sleep without fail. Next morning, no doubt, I would awake with the feeling of an old citizen.

"Before I acquire that," I replied, "I must know a little more about the sort of Boston I have come back to. You told me when we were upon the housetop that though a century only had elapsed since I fell asleep, it had been marked by greater changes in the conditions of humanity than many a previous millennium. With the city before me I could well believe that, but I am very curious to know what some of the changes have been. To make a beginning somewhere, for the subject is doubtless a large one, what solution, if any, have you found for the labour question? It was the Sphinx's riddle of the nineteenth century, and when I dropped out, the Sphinx was threatening to devour society because the answer was not forthcoming. It is well worth sleeping a hundred years to learn what the right answer was, if, indeed, you have found it yet."

"As no such thing as the labour question is known nowadays," replied Dr. Leete, "and there is no way in which it could arise, I suppose we may claim to have solved it. Society would indeed have fully deserved being devoured if it had failed to answer a riddle so entirely simple. In fact, to speak by the book, it was not necessary for society to solve the riddle at all. It may be said to have solved itself. The solution came as the result of a process of industrial evolution which could not have terminated otherwise. All that society had to do was to recognize and cooperate with that evolution, when its tendency had become unmistakable."

"I can only say", I answered, "that at the time I fell asleep no such evolution had been recognized."

"It was in 1887 that you fell into this sleep, I think you said."

"Yes, May 30th, 1887."

My companion regarded me musingly for some moments. Then he observed, "And you tell me that even then there was no general recognition of the nature of the crisis which society was nearing? Of course, I fully credit your statement. The singular blindness of your contemporaries to the signs of the times is a phenomenon commented on by many of our historians, but few facts of history are more difficult for us to realize, so obvious and unmistakable as we look back seem the indications, which must also have come under your eyes, of the transformation about to come to pass. I should be interested, Mr. West, if you would give me a little more definite idea of the view which you and men of your grade of intellect took of the state and prospects of society in 1887. You must at least have realized that the widespread industrial and social troubles, and the underlying dissatisfaction of all classes with the inequalities of society, and the general misery of mankind, were portents of great changes of some sort."

"We did, indeed, fully realize that", I replied. "We felt that society was dragging anchor and in danger of going adrift. Whither it would drift nobody could say, but all feared the rocks."

"Nevertheless," said Dr. Leete, "the set of the current was perfectly perceptible if you had but taken pains to observe it, and it was not towards the rocks, but towards a deeper channel."

"We had a popular proverb", I replied, "that 'hindsight is better than foresight', the force of which I shall now, no doubt, appreciate more fully than ever. All I can say is, that the prospect was such when I went into that long sleep that I should not have been surprised had I looked down from your housetop today on a heap of charred and moss-grown ruins instead of this glorious city."

Dr. Leete had listened to me with close attention and nodded thoughtfully as I finished speaking. "What you have said", he observed, "will be regarded as a most valuable vindication of Storiot, whose account of your era has been generally thought exaggerated in its picture of the gloom and confusion of men's minds. That a period of transition like that should be full of excitement and agitation was indeed to be looked for; but seeing how plain was the tendency of the forces in operation, it was natural to believe that hope rather than fear would have been the prevailing temper of the popular mind."

"You have not yet told me what was the answer to the riddle which you found", I said. "I am impatient to know by what contradiction of natural sequence the peace and prosperity which you now seem to enjoy could have been the outcome of an era like my own."

. . . "Since you are in the humour to talk rather than to sleep, as I certainly am, perhaps I cannot do better than to try to give you enough idea of our modern industrial system to dissipate at least the impression that there is any mystery about the process of its evolution. The Bostonians of your day had the reputation of being great askers of questions, and I am going to show my descent by asking you one to begin with. What should you name as the most prominent feature of the labour troubles of your day?"

"Why, the strikes, of course", I replied.

"Exactly, but what made the strikes so formidable?"

"The great labour organization."

"And what was the motive of these great organizations?"

"The workmen claimed they had to organize to get their rights from the big corporations", I replied.

"That is just it," said Dr. Leete, "the organization of labour and the strikes were an effect, merely, of the concentration of capital in greater masses than had ever been known before. Before this concentration began, while as yet commerce and industry were conducted by innumerable petty concerns with small capital, instead of a small number of great concerns with vast capital, the individual workman was relatively important and independent in his relations to the employer. Moreover, when a little capital or a new idea was enough to start a man in business for himself, working-men were constantly becoming employers, and there was no hard and fast line between the two classes. Labour unions were needless then, and general strikes out of the question. But when the era of small concerns with small capital was succeeded by that of the great aggregations of capital, all this was changed. The individual labourer, who had been relatively important to the small employer, was reduced to insignificance and powerlessness over against the great corporation, while at the same time the way upward to the grade of employer was closed to him. Self-defense drove him to union with his fellows.

"The records of the period show that the outcry against the concentration of capital was furious. Men believed that it threatened society with a form of tyranny more abhorrent than it had ever endured. They believed that the great corporations were preparing for them the yoke of a baser servitude than had ever been imposed on the race, servitude not to men but to soulless machines incapable of any motive but insatiable greed. Looking back, we cannot wonder at their desperation, for certainly humanity was never confronted with a fate more sordid and hideous than would have been the era of corporate tyranny which they anticipated.

"Meanwhile, without being in the smallest degree checked by the clamour against it, the absorption of business by ever larger monopolies continued. In the United States, where this tendency was later in developing than in Europe, there was not, after the beginning of the last quarter of the century, any opportunity whatever for individual enterprise in any important field of industry, unless backed by great capital. During the last decade of the century, such small businesses as still remained were fast-failing survivals of a past epoch or mere parasites on the great corporation, or else existed in fields too small to attract the great capitalists. Small businesses, as far as they still remained, were reduced to the condition of rats and mice, living in holes and corners, and counting on evading notice for the enjoyment of existence. The railroads had gone on combining till a few great syndicates controlled every rail in the land. In manufactories, every important staple was controlled by a syndicate. These syndicates, pools, trusts, or whatever their name, fixed prices and crushed all competition except when combinations as vast as themselves arose. Then a struggle, resulting in a still greater consolidation, ensued. The great city bazaar crushed its country rivals with branch stores, and in the city itself absorbed its smaller rivals till the business of a whole quarter was concentrated under one roof, with a hundred former proprietors of shops serving as clerks. Having no business of his own to put his money in, the small capitalist, at the same time that he took service under the corporation, found no other investment for his money but its stocks and bonds, thus becoming doubly dependent upon it.

"The fact that the desperate popular opposition to the consolidation of business in a few powerful hands had no effect to check it proves that there must have been a strong economical reason for it. The small capitalists, with their innumerable petty concerns, had in fact yielded the field to the great aggregations of capital, because they belonged to a day of small things and were totally incompetent to the demands of an age of steam and telegraphs and the gigantic scale of its enterprises. To restore the former order of things, even if possible, would have involved returning to the day of stagecoaches. Oppressive and intolerable as was the regime of the great consolidations of capital, even its victims, while they cursed it, were forced to admit the prodigious increase of efficiency which had been imparted to the national industries, the vast economies effected by concentration of management and unity of organization, and to confess that since the new system had taken the place of the old, the wealth of the world had increased at a rate before undreamt of. To be sure, this vast increase had gone chiefly to make the rich richer, increasing the gap between them and the poor; but the fact remained that, as a means merely of producing wealth, capital had been proved efficient in proportion to its consolidation. The restoration of the old system with the subdivision of capital, if it were possible, might indeed bring back a greater equality of conditions with more individual dignity and freedom, but it would be at the price of general poverty and the arrest of material progress.

"Was there, then, no way of commanding the services of the mighty wealth-producing principle of consolidated capital, without bowing down to a plutocracy like that of Carthage? As soon as men began to ask themselves these questions, they found the answer ready for them. The movement towards the conduct of business by larger and larger aggregations of capital, the tendency towards monopolies, which had been so desperately and vainly resisted, was recognized at last, in its true significance, as a process which only needed to complete its logical evolution to open a golden future to humanity.

"Early in the last century the evolution was completed by the final consolidation of the entire capital of the nation. The industry and commerce of the country, ceasing to be conducted by a set of irresponsible corporations and syndicates of private persons at their caprice and for their profit, were entrusted to a single syndicate representing the people, to be conducted in the common interest for the common profit. The nation, that is to say, organized as the one great business corporation in which all other corporations were absorbed; it became the one capitalist in the place of all other capitalists, the sole employer, the final monopoly in which all previous and lesser monopolies were swallowed up, a monopoly in the profits and economies of which all citizens shared. The epoch of trusts had ended in The Great Trust. In a word, the people of the United States concluded to assume the conduct of their own business, just as one hundred-odd years before they had assumed the conduct of their own government, organizing now for industrial purposes on precisely the same grounds that they had then organized for political purposes. At last, strangely late in the world's history, the obvious fact was perceived that no business is so essentially the public business as the industry and commerce on which the people's livelihood depends, and that to entrust it to private persons to be managed for private profit is a folly similar in kind, though vastly greater in magnitude, to that of surrendering the functions of political government to kings and nobles to be conducted for their personal glorification."

"Such a stupendous change as you describe", said I, "did not, of course, take place without great bloodshed and terrible convulsions."

"On the contrary," replied Dr. Leete, "there was absolutely no violence. The change had been long foreseen. Public opinion had become fully ripe for it, and the whole mass of the people was behind it. There was no more possibility of opposing it by force than by argument. On the other hand, the popular sentiment towards the great corporations and those identified with them had ceased to be one of bitterness, as they came to realize their necessity as a link, a transition phase, in the evolution of the true industrial system. The most violent foes of the great private monopolies were now forced to recognize how invaluable and indispensable had been their office in educating the people up to the point of assuming control of their own business. Fifty years before, the consolidation of the industries of the country under national control would have seemed a very daring experiment to the most sanguine. But by a series of object lessons, seen and studied by all men, the great corporations had taught the people an entirely new set of ideas on this subject. They had seen for many years syndicates handling revenues greater than those of states, and directing the labours of hundreds of thousands of men with an efficiency and economy unattainable in smaller operations. It had come to be recognized as an axiom that the larger the business the simpler the principles that can be applied to it; that, as the machine is truer than the hand, so the system, which in a great concern does the work of the master's eye in a small business, turns out more accurate results. Thus it came about that, thanks to the corporations themselves, when it was proposed that the nation should assume their functions, the suggestion implied nothing which seemed impracticable even to the timid. To be sure, it was a step beyond any yet taken, a broader generalization, but the very fact that the nation would be the sole corporation in the field would, it was seen, relieve the undertaking of many difficulties with which the partial monopolies had contended."

Looking Backward "The Great Trust"

LIFELONG EDUCATION

I n speaking of our educational system as it is at present," the doctor went on, "I should guard you against the possible mistake of supposing that the course which ends at twenty-one completes the educational curriculum of the average individual. On the contrary, it is only the required minimum of culture which society insists that all youth shall receive during their minority to make them barely fit for citizenship. We should consider it a very meager education indeed that ended there. As we look at it, the graduation from the schools at the attainment of majority means merely that the graduate has reached an age at which he can be presumed to be competent, and has the right as an adult to carry on his further education without the guidance or compulsion of the state. To provide means for this end the nation maintains a vast system of what you would call elective post-graduate courses of study in every branch of science, and these are open freely to everyone to the end of life, to be pursued as long or as briefly, as constantly or as intermittently, as profoundly or superficially, as desired.

"The mind is really not fit for . . . the most important branches of knowledge, the taste for them does not awake, and the intellect is not able to grasp them, until mature life, when a month of application will give a comprehension of a subject which years would have been wasted in trying to impart to a youth. It is our idea, so far as possible, to postpone the serious study of such branches to the post-graduate schools. Young people must get a smattering of things in general, but really theirs is not the time of life for ardent and effective study. If you would see enthusiastic students to whom the pursuit of knowledge is the greatest joy of life, you must seek them among the middle-aged fathers and mothers in the post-graduate schools.

"For the proper use of these opportunities for the lifelong pursuit of knowledge we find the leisure of our lives, which seems to you so ample, all too small. And yet that leisure, vast as it is, with half of every day and half of every year and the whole latter half of life sacred to personal uses — even the aggregate of these great spaces, growing greater with every labour-saving invention, which are reserved for the higher uses of life, would seem to us of little value for intellectual culture but for a condition commanded by almost none in your day, but secured to all by our institutions. I mean the moral atmosphere of serenity resulting from an absolute freedom of mind from disturbing anxieties and carking cares concerning our material welfare or that of those dear to us. Our economic system puts us in a position where we can follow Christ's maxim, so impossible for you, to 'take no thought for the morrow'. You must not understand, of course, that all our people are students or philosophers, but you may understand that we are more or less assiduous and systematic students and schoolgoers all our lives."

"Really, doctor," I said, "I do not understand that you have ever told me anything that has suggested a more complete and striking contrast between your age and mine than this about the persistent and growing development of the purely intellectual interests through life. In my day there was, after all, only six or eight years' difference in the duration of the intellectual life of the poor man's son drafted into the factory at fourteen and the more fortunate youth who went to college. If that of the one stopped at fourteen, that of the other ceased about as completely at twenty-one or twenty-two. Instead of being in a position to begin his real education on graduating from college, that event meant the close of it for the average student, and was the highwater mark of his life, so far as concerned the culture and knowledge of the sciences and humanities. In these respects the average college man never afterward knew so much as on his graduation day. For immediately thereafter, unless of the richest class, he must needs plunge into the turmoil and strife of business life, and engage in the struggle for the material means of existence. Whether he failed or succeeded made little difference as to the effect to stunt and wither his intellectual life. He had no time and could command no thought for anything else. If he failed, or barely avoided failure, perpetual anxiety ate out his heart; and if he succeeded, his success usually made him a grosser and more hopelessly self-satisfied materialist than if he had failed. There was no hope for his mind or soul either way. If at the end of life his efforts had won him a little breathing space, it could be of no high use to him, for the spiritual and intellectual parts had become atrophied from disuse, and were no longer capable of responding to opportunity."

"And this apology for an existence", said the doctor, "was the life of those whom you counted most fortunate and most successful — of those who were reckoned to have won the prizes of life. Can you be surprised that we look back to the great Revolution as a sort of second creation of man, inasmuch as it added the conditions of an adequate mind and soul life to the bare physical existence under more or less agreeable conditions, which was about all the life the most of human beings, rich or poor, had up to that time known? The effect of the struggle for existence in arresting, with its engrossments, the intellectual development at the very threshold of adult life would have been disastrous enough had the character of the struggle been morally unobjectionable. It is when we come to consider that the struggle was one which not only prevented mental culture, but was utterly withering to the moral life, that we fully realize the unfortunate condition of the race before the Revolution. Youth is visited with noble aspirations and high dreams of duty and perfection. It sees the world as it should be, not as it is; and it is well for the race if the institutions of society are such as do not offend these moral enthusiasms, but rather tend to conserve and develop them through life. This, I think, we may fully claim the modern social order does. Thanks to an economic system which illustrates the highest ethical idea in all its workings, the youth going forth into the world finds it a practical school for all the moralities. He finds full room and scope in its duties and occupations for every generous enthusiasm, every unselfish aspiration he ever cherished. He cannot possibly have formed a moral idea higher or completer than that which dominates our industrial and commercial order.

"Youth was as noble in your day as now, and dreamt the same great dreams of life's possibilities. But when the young man went forth into the world of practical life it was to find his dreams mocked and his ideals derided at every turn. He found himself compelled, whether he would or not, to take part in a fight for life, in which the first condition of success was to put his ethics on the shelf and cut the acquaintance of his conscience. You had various terms with which to describe the process whereby the young man, reluctantly laying aside his ideals, accepted the conditions of the sordid struggle. You described it as a 'learning to take the world as it is', 'getting over romantic notions', 'becoming practical', and all that. In fact, it was nothing more nor less than the debauching of a soul. Is that too much to say?"

"It is no more than the truth, and we all knew it", I answered. "Thank God, that day is over forever! The father need now no longer instruct the son in cynicism lest he should fail in life, nor the mother her daughter in worldly wisdom as a protection from generous instinct. The parents are worthy of their children and fit to associate with them, as it seems to us they were not and could not be in your day. Life is all the way through as spacious and noble as it seems to the ardent child standing on the threshold. The ideals of perfection, the enthusiasms of self-devotion, honour, love and duty, which thrill the boy and girl, no longer yield with advancing years to baser motives, but continue to animate life to the end. You remember what Wordsworth said:

> Heaven lies about us in our infancy!
> Shades of the prison-house begin to close
> Upon the growing boy.

I think if he were a partaker of our life he would not have been moved to extol childhood at the expense of maturity, for life grows ever wider and higher to the last."

Equality, Chapter XXX

WHY A NEW NATION?

W
hy a New Nation? Why will not the old one do? These
are some of the reasons why it will not do: In the old
nation, the system by which the work of life is carried
on is a sort of perpetual warfare, a struggle, literally to the death,
between men and men. It is a system by which the contestants are
forced to waste in fighting more effort than they have left for
work. The sordid and bitter nature of the struggle so hardens, for
the most part, the relations of men to their fellows that in the
domestic circle alone do they find exercise for the better, tenderer
and more generous elements of their nature.

Another reason why the old nation will not do is that in it the
people are divided, against nature, into classes: one very small
class being the wealthy; another and much larger class being
composed of those who maintain with difficulty a condition of
tolerable comfort constantly shadowed by apprehension of its loss;
with, finally, a vastly greater and quite preponderating class of
very poor, who have no dependence even for a bare existence save
a wage which is uncertain from day to day.

In the old nation, moreover, half the people, the women, are
dependent upon the other half, the men, for the means of support;
no other alternative being left them but to seek a beggarly pittance
as workers in a labour market already overcrowded by men. In
this old nation, the women are, indeed, as a sex, far worse off than
the men; for, while the rich man is at least independent, the rich
woman, while more luxuriously cared for, is as dependent for
support on her husband's favour as the wife of the poorest
labourer. Meanwhile, a great many women openly, and no one
can tell how many secretly, unable to find men who will support
them on more honourable terms, are compelled to secure their
livelihood by the sale of their bodies, while a multitude of others
are constrained to accept loveless marriage bonds.

In this old nation, a million strong men are even now vainly
crying out for work to do, though the world needs so much more
work done. Meanwhile, though the fathers and husbands can find
no work, there is plenty always for the little children, who flock, in

piteous armies, through the chilling mists of winter dawns into the factories.

In this old nation, not only does wealth devour poverty, but wealth devours wealth, and, year by year, the assets of the nation pass more swiftly and completely into the hands of a few score individuals out of sixty-five million people.

In this old nation, year by year, the natural wealth of the land, the heritage of the people, is being wasted by the recklessness of individual greed. The forests are ravaged, the fisheries of river and sea destroyed, the fertility of the soil exhausted.

In this old nation, under a vain form of free political institutions, the inequalities of wealth and the irresistible influence of money upon a people devoured by want are making nominally republican institutions a machine more convenient even than despotism for the purposes of plutocracy and plunder.

These are a few of the reasons why the old nation will not do, and these, in turn, are a few of the reasons why men are looking and longing for The New Nation:

In The New Nation work will not be warfare, but fraternal cooperation towards a store in which all will share alike. Human effort, no longer wasted by battle and cross purposes, will create an abundance previously impossible.

More important far, the conditions of labour under the plan of fraternal cooperation will tend as strongly to stimulate fraternal sentiments and affectionate relations among the workers as the present conditions tend to repress them. The kindly side of men will no longer be known only to their wives and children.

In The New Nation, there will be neither rich nor poor; all will be equal partners in the product of the national industrial organization.

In The New Nation, the dependence of one sex upon another for livelihood, which now poisons love and gives lust its opportunity, will be forever at an end. As equal and independent partners in the product of the nation, women will have attained an economical enfranchisement, without which no political device could help them. Prostitution will be a forgotten horror.

In The New Nation, there will be no unemployed. All will be enabled and required to do their part according to their gifts, save only those whom age, sickness or infirmity has exempted; and these, no longer as now trodden underfoot, will be served and guarded as tenderly as are the wounded in battle by their comrades.

In The New Nation, the children will be cherished as precious jewels, inestimable pledges of the divine love to men. Though mother and father forsake them, the nation will take them up.

In The New Nation, education will be equal and universal, and will cover the entire period of life during which it is now enjoyed by the most favoured classes.

In The New Nation, the wasting of the people's heritage will cease, the forests will be replanted, the rivers and seas repopulated and fertility restored to exhausted lands. The natural resources of the country will be cared for and preserved as a common estate, and one to which the living have title only as trustees for the unborn.

In The New Nation, the debauching influence of wealth being banished, and the people raised to a real equality by equal education and resources, a true democratic and popular government will become possible as it never was before. For the first time in history the world will behold a true republic, rounded, full orbed, complete — a republic, social, industrial, political.

The New Nation, January 1894

DECLARATION OF PRINCIPLES

The principle of the Brotherhood of Humanity is one of the eternal truths that govern the world's progress on lines which distinguish human nature from brute nature. The principle of competition is simply the application of the brutal law of the survival of the strongest and most cunning.

Therefore, so long as competition continues to be the ruling factor in our industrial system, the highest development of the individual cannot be reached, the loftiest aims of humanity cannot be realized.

No truth can avail unless practically applied. Therefore, those who seek the welfare of man must endeavour to suppress the system founded on the brute principle of competition and put in its place another based on the nobler principle of association.

But in striving to apply this nobler and wiser principle to the complex conditions of modern life, we advocate no sudden or ill-considered changes; we make no war upon individuals; we do not censure those who have accumulated immense fortunes simply by carrying to a logical end the false principle on which business is now based.

The combinations, trusts and syndicates of which the people at present complain demonstrate the practicability of our basic principle of association. We merely seek to push this principle a little further and have all industries operated in the interest of all by the nation — the people organized — the organic unity of the whole people.

The present industrial system proves itself wrong by the immense wrongs it produces; it proves itself absurd by the immense waste of energy and material which is admitted to be its concomitant. Against this system we raise our protest; for the abolition of the slavery it has wrought and would perpetuate, we pledge our best efforts.

The Nationalist, May 1889

NATIONALISM —
PRINCIPLES AND PURPOSES

No fact is better established by experience or more easily demonstrable by reason than that no republic can long exist unless a substantial equality in the wealth of citizens prevails. Wealth is power in its most concentrated, most efficient and most universally applicable form. In the presence of great disparities of wealth, social equality is at an end, industrial independence is destroyed, while mere constitutional stipulations as to the equal rights of citizens politically or before the law become ridiculous.

One hundred years ago this republic was founded upon a substantial equality in the condition of the people. It was not an equality established by law, but a condition resulting from a general state of poverty. For the first fifty years the increase in the wealth of the country was gradual, but within the last thirty years, owing to great mechanical and commercial inventions, it has multiplied by leaps and bounds, no longer growing from decade to decade by arithmetical, but by geometrical ratio. Instead of chiefly tending to enhance the general welfare of the people, this wealth has been mainly appropriated by a small class. At the present time the property of one hundred thousand men in the United States aggregates more than the total possessions of the rest of the people. Ten thousand people own nearly the whole of New York City with its two million population. The entire bonded debt of the United States is held by seventy-one thousand persons only, and over sixty percent of it is in the hands of twenty-three thousand persons. A volume of similar details might be furnished, but the situation may be summed up in one of the characteristic phrases of modern business, as follows: Mainly within thirty years one hundred thousand Americans have succeeded in 'freezing out' their sixty-five million co-partners as to more than half the assets of the concern, and at the rate of the last thirty years, within thirty years more will have secured the remainder.

That is the situation which has created the need for Nationalism. Those are the facts which account for the rapidity of its spread among the people.

For the sake of clearness let us distinguish the evil effects of the concentration of wealth in the hands of a few, as political, social and industrial. First as to the political effects. The great corporations and combinations of capital dwarf our municipalities, overtop our states and are able to dictate to our national legislature. The extent to which intimidation and bribery are employed to influence popular elections taints with the suspicion of fraud nearly all verdicts of the ballot when the majority is not large. Even in the grand appeal to the nation the money power, by judicious concentration of corruption funds upon close states, is able to set at naught the will of the people. The titles of the presidents of the republic are no longer clear. What money cannot effect at the polls, by intimidation or by bribery, it does not hesitate to attempt by the corruption of individual legislators. Our municipal council chambers are too often mere auction rooms, where public franchises are sold to the highest briber. The legislatures of some of our greatest states are commonly said to be owned by particular corporations. The United States Senate is known as a "rich men's club", and in the lower house of Congress the schemes of capital have only to meet the sham opposition of the demagogue.

Socially, the vast disparities of wealth afford on every side inhuman contrasts of cruel want and inordinate luxury. The dazzling illustrations of pomp and power, which are the prizes of wealth, have lent to the pursuit of gain, at all times sufficiently keen, a feverish intensity and desperation never seen before in this or any other country. The moderate rewards of persistent industry seem contemptible in the midst of a universal speculative fever. In all directions the old ways of legitimate business and steady application are being abandoned for speculative projects, gambling operations and all manner of brigandage under forms of law. The spectacle presented in many instances of great riches, notoriously won by corrupt methods, has undermined the foundations of honesty. The epidemic of fraud and embezzlement, which today renders wealth so insecure, results from the general recognition that the possession of property, though it may have a legal title, is very commonly without a moral one. This is the deplorable explanation of the cynical tolerance of fraud by public opinion. Property will not, in the long run, be respected which is without some reasonable basis in industry or desert, and it is justly believed that much of the wealth of today could not stand enquiry into the means of its getting.

The consequences of the appropriation of the nation's wealth by a few, and its further concentration by means of corporations and syndicates, have made possible a policy of monopolizing the control and profits of the industries of the country never before even imagined as among the possible perils of society. Hitherto, when oligarchies have usurped the political control of nations, they have left the conduct of business to the vulgar, but our new order of 'nobility' is laying its foundations deeper by obtaining absolute mastery of the means of support of the people.

The effect of the concentration and combination of capital in the conduct of business has been directly to bring the wage-earner more completely than ever under the thumb of the employer. A chief object of combination is to control prices by restricting production — that is to say, employment. While the competition among wage-earners for work is thus made more desperate, they are placed at the mercy of employers by the fact that in so far as employers are consolidated they no longer compete with one another.

But there could be no greater mistake than to fancy that the manual worker is peculiarly a victim of the present situation. The business men, the small tradesmen and manufacturers and the professional classes are suffering quite as much and have quite as much to dread from monopoly as has the poorest class of labourers.

As one after another the different departments of business, productive and distributive, pass under the single or syndicate control of the great capitalists, the so-called middle class, the business men with moderate capital and plenty of wit, who used to conduct the business of the country, are crowded out of their occupation and rendered superfluous. No doubt the substitution of single for multiple control and the suppression of middlemen represents an economy. But the economy does not benefit the consumer, but goes to swell the profits of the capitalists.

Meanwhile, fathers who were set up by their fathers in business find it impossible to do the like for their sons. There is now almost no opportunity left for starting in business in a moderate way; none, indeed, unless backed by large capital. What this means is that we are rapidly approaching a time when there will be no class between the very rich, living on their capital, and a vast mass of wage and salary receivers absolutely dependent upon the former class for their livelihood. Meanwhile, as the immediate effect of the closing up of business careers to young men, the professions are being overcrowded to the starvation point. The problem before young men coming out of school or college, where to find a place in the world, was never so hard as now. Plutocracy is indeed fast leaving no place for a young man of independent and patriotic spirit, save in the party of Radical Social Reform.

The agricultural interests of the country are passing under the yoke of the money power quite as rapidly as the other forms of industry. The farmers are becoming expropriated by the operation of something like a universal mortgage system, and unless this tendency shall be checked the next generation of farmers will be a generation of tenants-at-will. The agrarian conditions of Ireland bid fair in no long time to be reproduced in portions of the West.

Such, fellow countrymen, is the condition of political corruption, of social rottenness, of moral degeneracy, of industrial oppression, confusion and impending ruin which has resulted from the overthrow of our republican equality by the money power. If you would learn how republics perish, shut up your musty histories of Greece and Rome and look about you.

In time the money power is bound to seek protection from the rising discontent of the masses in a stronger form of government, and then the republic, long before dead, will be put out of sight. Then it will be too late to resist. Now it is not too late. The republic is being taken from us, but it is still possible to bring it back. Soon it will be too late to do so, but today there is yet time, though there is none to waste.

The Nationalists of the United States ask the cooperation of their fellow countrymen to bring back the republic. To that end they propose a reorganization of the industrial system which shall restore the equality of the people and secure it by a perpetual guarantee.

In advocating a plan to secure equality we propose to graft no new or strange principle upon the republican idea, but the exercise of a power implied in the very idea of republicanism as ultimately necessary to its preservation. A republic is a form of government based upon and guaranteeing to all citizens a common interest in the national concern. That interest can be common only in proportion as it is substantially an equality of interest. The time has now come in America, as it has come sooner or later in the history of all republics, when by the increase of wealth and by gross disparity in its distribution, this equality in its three aspects — political, social, industrial — is threatened with complete subversion. In order, under the changed conditions, to make good the original pledge of the republic to its citizens, it has become necessary to re-establish and maintain by some deliberate plan that economic equality, the basis of all other sorts of equality which, when the republic was established, existed in a substantial degree by nature. The question is not of assuming a new obligation, but whether the original ends and purposes of the republican compact shall be repudiated. We demand that the republic keep faith with the people, and propose a plan of industrial reorganization which seems to us the only possible means by which that faith can be kept. We are the true conservative party, because we are devoted to the maintenance of republican institutions against the revolution now being effected by the money power. We propose no revolution, but that the people shall resist a revolution. We oppose those who are overthrowing the republic. Let no mistake be made here. We are not revolutionists, but counter-revolutionists.

But while the guarantee of the equality of citizens is thus a measure amply justified and necessitated by merely patriotic and national considerations, without looking further for arguments, we do, in proposing this action, look both further and higher, to the ends of the earth, indeed, and the ultimate destiny of the race.

While historic, political and economic conditions require that this movement should be conducted on national lines by each people for itself, we hold the economic equality of all men a principle of universal application, having for its goal the eventual establishment of a brotherhood of humanity as wide as the world and as numerous as mankind. Those who believe that all men are brothers, and should so regard one another, must believe in the equality of men, for equals only can be brothers. Even brothers by blood do but hate each other the more bitterly for the tie when the inheritance is unequally parted between them, while strangers are presently made to feel like brothers by equality of interest and community of loss and gain. Therefore we look to the establishment of equality among men as the physical basis necessary to realize that brotherhood of humanity regarded by the good and wise of all ages as the ideal state of society. We believe that a wonderful confluence, at the present epoch, of material and moral tendencies throughout the world, but especially in America, has made a great step in the evolution of humanity, not only possible, but necessary for the salvation of the race. We are surrounded by perils from which the only way of escape is the way upward.

The plan of industrial reorganization which Nationalism proposes is the very simple and obvious one of placing the industrial duty of citizens on the ground on which their military duty already rests. All able-bodied citizens are held bound to fight for the nation, and, on the other hand, the nation is bound to protect all citizens, whether they are able to fight or not. Why not extend this accepted principle to industry, and hold every able-bodied citizen bound to work for the nation, whether with mind or muscle, and, on the other hand, hold the nation bound to guarantee the livelihood of every citizen, whether able to work or not. As in military matters the duty to fight is conditioned upon physical ability, while the right of protection is conditioned only upon citizenship, so would we condition the obligation to work upon the strength to work, but the right to support upon citizenship only.

The result would be to substitute for the present ceaseless industrial civil war, of which it would be hard to say whether it is more brutal or more wasteful, a partnership of all the people, a great joint stock company to carry on the business of the country for the benefit of all equally, women with men, sick with well, strong with weak. This plan of a national business partnership of equals we hold not only to be demonstrably practicable, but to constitute as truly the only scientific plan for utilizing the energy of the people in wealth production, as it is the only basis for society consistent with justice, with the sentiment of brotherhood, with the teachings of the founder of Christianity, and, indeed, of the founders of all the great religions.

The realization of the proposed plan of industry requires as the preliminary step the acquisition by the nation through its government, national and municipal, of the present industrial machinery of the country. It follows, therefore, that the Nationalists' programme must begin with the progressive nationalization of the industries of the United States. In proposing this course we are animated by no sentiment of bitterness towards individuals or classes. In antagonizing the money power we antagonize not men but a system. We advocate no rash or violent measures, nor such as will produce derangement of business or undue hardship to individuals. We aim to change the law by the law, and the Constitution, if necessary, by constitutional methods. As to the order in which industries should be nationalized, priority should naturally be given to those the great wealth of which renders them perilous to legislative independence, to those which deal extortionately with the public or oppressively with employees, to those which are highly systematized and centralized and to those which can be readily assimilated by existing departments of government.

The following are some of the measures in the line of this policy for which the country appears to be quite ready:

First — The nationalization of the railroads whether by constituting the United States perpetual receiver of all lines, to manage the same for the public interest, paying over to the present security-holders, pending the complete establishment of Nationalism, such reasonable dividends on a just valuation of the property as may be earned, or by some other practicable method not involving hardship to individuals.

The nationalization of railroads is advisable for reasons apart from the Nationalist programme proper. Firstly, the railroad corporations, by the corrupt use of their vast wealth to procure and prevent legislation, are among the most formidable of the influences which are debauching our government. Secondly, the power they wield irresponsibly over the prosperity of cities, states and entire sections of the country ought to be in the hands only of the general government. Thirdly, the desperate rivalry of the railroads, with its incidents of reckless extension, duplication and rate wars, has long been a chief waste of the national resources and a cause of periodical business crises. Fourthly, the financial management of a large portion of the railroad system, together with its use for speculative purposes, has rendered railroad financiering the most gigantic gambling and general swindling business ever carried on in any country. Fifthly, the convenience and safety of the travelling public demand a uniform and harmonious railroad system throughout the country, nor is it likely that anything less will bring to an end the cruel slaughter of railroad employees now carried on by the corporations.

A second measure for which the people are certainly quite ready is the nationalization of the telegraphic and telephone services, and their addition to the post office, with which, as departments of transmission of intelligence, they should properly always have been connected.

Third — We propose that the express business of the country be assumed by the post offices, according to the successful practices of other countries.

Fourth — We propose that the coal-mining business which at present is most rapaciously conducted as respects the public, and most oppressively as regards a great body of labourers, be nationalized, to the end that the mines may be continuously worked to their full capacity, coal furnished consumers at cost and the miners humanely dealt with. It is suggested that all mines hereafter discovered or opened shall be regarded as public property subject to just compensation for land.

Fifth — We propose that municipalities generally shall undertake lighting, heating, running of streetcars and such other municipal services as are now discharged by corporations, to the end that such services may be more cheaply and effectually rendered; that a fruitful source of political corruption be cut off and a large body of labourers be brought under humaner conditions of toil.

Pending the municipalization of all such services as have been referred to, Nationalists enter a general protest against the grant to corporations of any further franchises whether relating to transit, light, heat, water or other public services.

It is to be understood that all nationalized and municipalized businesses should be conducted at cost for use and not for profit, the amount at present paid in taxes by such businesses being, however, charged upon them.

It is an essential feature of the method of Nationalism that as fast as industries are nationalized or municipalized, the conditions of the workers in them shall be placed upon a wholly humane basis. The hours of labour will be made reasonable, the compensation adequate, the conditions safe and healthful. Support in sickness, with pensions for disabled and superannuated workers, will be guaranteed.

The question will be asked, "How is this great force of public employees to be placed beyond the power of politicians and administrations to use for partisan purposes?" Nationalists respond by proposing a plan for organizing and maintaining all public departments of business that shall absolutely deprive parties or politicians of any direct or arbitrary power over their membership, either as to appointment, promotion or removal.

In the first place, it is understood that upon the nationalization of any business the existing force of employees and functionaries would be as a body retained. It is proposed that the service should be forthwith strictly graded and subsequently recruited exclusively by admissions to the lowest grade. All persons desiring to enter the service should be free to file applications at the proper bureau upon passing certain simple mental or physical tests, not competitive in character and adapted only to minimum grade of qualifications. Upon vacancies occurring in the force or a need of increase, the desired additions should be taken from the list of applicants on file, either in order of filed applications or, more perfectly to prevent fraud, by the drawing of the requisite number of names from a wheel containing the entire list of eligibles.

The chief of the department should be appointed at the discretion of the political executive, whether of city, state or nation, in order that responsibility for the general management of the business might be brought home to an elective officer. With this exception, and perhaps the further exceptions in some cases of the chiefs of a few important subordinate branches of the service, all positions should be filled by promotion in order of grades, such promotions to be determined by superiority of record and with certain requirements of length of service. While the chief should have power of suspension, no discharge from the service should take place save by verdict of a tribunal expressly erected for that purpose, before which all charges of fault or incompetence, whether by superior against subordinate, by subordinate against superior or by the outside public against members of the force, should be laid.

It is believed that such a plan of organization would absolutely prevent administrative coercion of members of the public service for partisan ends, and it is urgently recommended by Nationalists that it be immediately applied to the post office and all other business departments of the general government, to the employees and to the public works department of all municipalities.

The nationalization of the several great branches of public service and productions which have been enumerated would directly affect, greatly for the better, the condition of a million and a half workers.

Here truly would be a bulwark against capitalism, against corporate usurpation, against industrial oppression. Here would be a mighty nucleus for the coming industrial army. Here too, would be a great body of consumers whose needs would suggest and whose demands would sustain the beginning of the coming national distributive and productive system.

Even a single industry organized on such a basis as described and guaranteeing to its toilers security, health, safety, dignity and justice would be an object lesson of the advantage of Nationalism, even in its beginnings, which would greatly hasten the general adoption of the system. As a measure which cannot wait, seeing that, at best, the consequences of its postponement must continue to be felt long after it is effected, we urge that such partisan support as may be needful to enable them to attend school to the age of seventeen, at least, be provided under proper guards by the state for the children of parents unable to maintain them without aid from their labour, and that with this provision the employment of children should be unconditionally forbidden, and their education made rigidly compulsory, to the end that equality of educational opportunities for all be established.

Seeing that it would be manifestly inconsistent to make the education of our children compulsory while permitting the unlimited importation of adult ignorance and vice, a necessary complement to any system of education would be such regulation of foreign immigration as, without prejudice to honest intelligent poverty, should prevent the importation of persons grossly illiterate in their own language, of the defective and of criminals, merely political offenses not being considered crimes.

In reviewing the measures which have been mentioned as substantially representing, according to my belief, the present demands of Nationalists, it is observable that there is not one of them which is not demanded by considerations of humanity and public expediency quite without reference to Nationalism. A man has no need to be a Nationalist at all to advocate them. They have been freely and often favourably discussed by the press for years, and the leading political economists of this country and Europe are on record in favour of most if not all of them. As to some of the most important of these propositions, it is altogether probable that a majority of the American people, if they could be polled today, would favour them. Nationalists may be, as some say, a very extravagant and fantastical set of people, but there is certainly nothing fantastical about the plan of action which they propose. There is not even anything which can be said to be greatly in advance of public opinion. This moderation is not accidental, nor yet a result of policy, but a necessary consequence of the method of Nationalism, which is essentially gradual and progressive rather than abrupt or violent, the method of evolution as opposed to that of revolution.

As to the relation of Nationalism to certain political and social issues of the day, a few words may be pertinent.

First, as to the tariff question. When the nation conducts all business for all, the common interest in every improvement will create a far stronger motive than now exists for all sorts of experiments and improvements in home industry, but owing to the public control of the production, tariffs will no longer be necessary as now to encourage private persons to undertake such new experiments. They will be tried as government experiments are now tried, costing the country only the expense of the experimental stations, the nation without prejudice to the experiment continuing, if expedient, to buy in the cheapest market till its own is the cheapest.

The sectional jealousies based upon industrial rivalry, which now make states and cities enemies of each other's prosperity and create sentiments of disunion, will disappear when a national pooling of interests shall interest all equally in the prosperity of all.

As to the race issue, the industrial discipline imposed by Nationalism, while of general benefit to the white population of the South in common with that of the North, will be an ideal system for developing, guiding and elevating the recently emancipated coloured race. It should be distinctly stated that the national plan will put an end to every form of sexual slavery and place feminine freedom and dignity upon an unassailable basis by making women independent of men for the means of support. We consider that by no method less radical can women's rightful equality with men be established, or, if established, maintained.

The evils of intemperance have their strongest roots in the brutalizing conditions of existing society, in the poverty of the masses, their gross ignorance, their misery and despair, in the slavish dependence of women and children upon men, and in the interest of a large class of tradesmen in the sale of intoxicants. If this be true, then the abolition of poverty, the universality of the best education, the complete enfranchisement of women, with a system of distribution which will destroy all personal motive for stimulating the sale of intoxicants, constitute surely the most promising as well as the most radical line of true temperance reform.

While the nationalizing of land in such time and by such methods as shall involve least hardships to any is a part of the national plan, and while the Nationalists meanwhile favour all practicable measures to prevent land monopoly and protect tenants and farmers, they are not persuaded that any measure applying to land alone would furnish a sufficient remedy for existing industrial and social troubles.

While sympathizing with all efforts of workers to obtain small immediate improvements in their condition, Nationalists would have them reflect that no great improvements can be gained, and if gained, can be secure, under the present industrial system, and that the only effectual and peaceable way of replacing that system by a better one is offered by Nationalism. It is also pointed out that the plan of Nationalism, by the humane and just conditions which will be secured to the employees of every industry, as it comes under the public control, offers not only the greatest ultimate results, but the speediest and surest way for immediately benefitting great bodies of workers absolutely without risk of derangement of business.

One hundred years ago, after immemorial years of repression, the human passion for liberty, for equality, for brotherhood burst forth, convulsing Europe and establishing America. There is at hand another and far mightier outburst of the same forces, the results of which will be incomparably more profound, more far-reaching and more beneficent. Men now past middle age are likely to see in Europe the last throne fall, and in America the first complete and full-orbed republic arise, a republic at once political, industrial and social.

It is instructive for Americans to remember that there is scarcely any argument brought today against Nationalism which was not in substance brought against the experiment of political equality undertaken in this country a century ago; scarcely one which does not spring from the same low and suspicious estimate of human nature, the same distrust of the people, the same blind belief in personal and class leadership and authority; scarcely one which was not, as to principle, answered a hundred years ago by Madison, Hamilton and Jay in *The Federalist*. And, indeed, how could it be otherwise? For what we propose is but the full development of the same republican experiment which the fathers undertook, a development now become necessary if we would preserve that experiment from ignominious failure.

In advocating equal rights for all as the only solution for the social and industrial problems of today, Nationalism follows the lines laid down by the founders of the republic and proves itself the legitimate heir to the traditions and the spirit of 1776. Guided by those traditions, sustained by that spirit, we cannot fail.

Address At Tremont Temple, Boston
December 19, 1889

SOME MISCONCEPTIONS OF NATIONALISM

A hopeful sign for Nationalism is the fact that its opponents usually criticize it for what it is not, which suggests the possibility that they may become good Nationalists when they learn what it is. I propose very briefly, as must needs be in a paper of this length, to correct some of these misconceptions.

First. Nationalism is not based on the maxim "To each according to his needs, from each according to his abilities." Of course, as a matter of conscience, every man is bound to do all he can, and the needs of others are sacred claims upon his service; but both abilities and needs are indeterminate, and therefore could not be made the basis of any regulation to be enforced by society. The principle of Nationalism is: From all equally; to all equally. Nationalism will require of all not exempted by natural defect or inability an equal term of industrial service, using this expression as inclusive of all useful mental as well as physical effort. It is, of course, true that men will serve more or less efficiently according to their abilities, just as soldiers in military service do; but the terms of the industrial, as of the military service, the requirements made of the workers, as of soldiers, will be equal for all. Conversely, the nation will guarantee to citizens, both workers and those wholly or partially unable to work — strong with weak, women with men, sick with well — an equal maintenance. That is to say, Nationalism adopts the half-truth expressed in the old adage that the world owes everyone a living, but not without supplementing it with the other half of the truth — that everyone owes the world a reasonable service. Nationalists argue that it is the business of society to provide the machinery requisite for the discharge of these reciprocal obligations of the community and the individual, and believe that nothing but national cooperation will furnish that machinery.

It is worth consideration that, as between the workers, the provision for an equal maintenance, regardless of differences in personal efficiency, is not a new idea, but only the extension to all trades of the principle of a uniform rate of wages already prevailing by custom or by trade rule in very many occupations, skilled and unskilled. A large proportion of the trades unions find it necessary to enforce this rule very rigidly as the only way to secure harmony of interest, and consequently of feeling, among the membership of particular trades; and the same consideration, if no other, would render the extension of the same rule to all trades an indispensable condition to the stability of any system of national cooperation.

As to the proposition of Nationalism to extend the guarantee of an equal maintenance, not only to all workers, but to those also who are wholly or partially unable to work, such as the sick, the infirm and women, this too will be admitted, upon a moment's reflection, to be an innovation in form rather than in substance. The dependent classes now and always have been supported out of the earnings of the workers — some in luxury, some in penury, but all supported in some way. Nationalism will only average and systematize this support, without necessarily increasing the total cost to the workers, while, by abolishing the humiliating personal dependence of the weak and infirm upon the favour of the strong and well for the means of support, it will spare the self-respect of a class already sorely burdened by nature, to the incalculable gain in dignity and nobility of human relations.

Second. While Nationalism means that the strong shall bear the infirmities of the weak, it does not mean that the industrious shall support the idle. On the contrary, for the first time in human history, it will take the lazy off the backs of the willing and compel them to support themselves, if not by voluntary labour, then by involuntary.

Third. But, granting the suppression of idleness, will not equality of maintenance on the part of all workers leave less motive to strenuous exertion than the pursuit of wealth now calls forth? The reply is that mutual emulation, the desire of approbation and the ambition for name and prominence are the real motives which, thinly disguised under the name of love of money, at present prompt the bulk of the world's work, and all its good work. These motives would not only be preserved but greatly intensified under Nationalism which would make the ranks, dignities, offices and honours, from lowest to highest, of the industrial service and of the state, with the social distinction corresponding to them, exclusively the prizes of superior diligence and achievement. Since all would gain equally by efficiency in the public service, the public interest would imperatively demand that the career should be open to talent as it never had been before. *Fourth.* But will not Nationalism discourage individuality? Let us see. At present the vast majority of persons do not receive education enough to find out what their individual qualities and aptitudes are. Even when these are discovered, there is no provision whatever for assisting the individual to secure the sort of work he prefers and is best fitted for. Chance and circumstance determine the fate of most. Warped faculties and stunted growth, round pegs in square holes and square pegs in round ones, are the natural results of these conditions. Finally, the dependence for employment of all workers, manual or intellectual, upon the favour of individuals, corporations, communities or groups of patrons, makes originality or independence of speech or conduct an indulgence involving the risk of livelihood for one's self and family. Fortunate are the few who have not felt the pressure of this sordid bondage.

Under Nationalism, on the contrary, the universal enjoyment of the best educational advantages might be depended on in the first place to provide opportunity for developing everyone's qualities and aptitudes — that is to say, for discovering his individuality. Seeing that under a national cooperative system every person not employed to the best advantage would be a public loss to the extent of the misfit, the utmost pains would be taken, as a measure of economy quite apart from moral motives, to see that everyone was helped to the kind of work he was best adapted to. Finally, no one would be dependent in any way as to livelihood upon the favour of any individual, group or community, however large, but would have his or her maintenance guaranteed by the constitution of the nation, not to be diminished or taken away during orderly behaviour by anything less than a revolution. Could conditions more favourable than these to the development of a robust individuality be imagined? So far will Nationalism be from discouraging individuality that it will constitute a school for developing it.

Owing to their dependence for maintenance upon the favour of men, which again is largely a reflection of public opinion, women are doubly the slaves of conventionality and need to be heroines to assert independence and individuality. As a consequence of this fact, the moral and intellectual development of the race has been incalculably retarded. By guaranteeing women economical independence of and equality with men as a corner-stone of its polity, Nationalism, in the only effectual way possible, will bring to pass the bodily, mental and moral enfranchisement of woman.

Fifth. An equal provision for maintenance does not mean a uniform mode of maintenance, or a similar manner of life, any more than the receipt of the same amount in wages, salary or income by two or more persons at the present day means that they must wear the same clothes, eat the same dishes or choose the same wall paper. If everybody wants to live like everybody else under Nationalism, of course they will be free to do so, but there will be no more reason why they should than there is today.

Much anxiety has been expressed lest equality of educational advantages and of incomes should make society dull and monotonous. The inference is that the educated, refined and well-to-do nowadays depend largely for entertainment upon their intercourse with the ignorant, the coarse and the poverty-stricken; that Fifth Avenue would die of ennui without the East Side. Is this true? Is it not true, on the contrary, that, socially speaking, like seeks like and that birds of a feather flock together, that comfort is offended by the sight of misery, that refinement is wounded by coarseness, and that the ideal of the intelligent is a society in which intelligence is universal?

Sixth. It is not proposed to realize the ideal of Nationalism by abrupt or revolutionary methods, but by the progressive nationalizing and municipalizing of existing public services and industries. It is proposed to begin by adding telegraph, telephone and express services to the post office, according to the successful practice of foreign nations, by nationalizing the railroads and the coal-mining business, and by the municipalizing of all services now discharged for towns and cities by corporations. In all these measures three ends will be aimed at: First, to put an end to the present wholesale debauching of legislative bodies by the wealthy corporations now profiting by the services in question. Second, the increase of the cheapness and efficiency of those services which will result from conducting them for public use instead of private profit and from making them directly amenable as to shortcomings to popular criticism. Third, a radical improvement in the condition of the workers in nationalized or municipalized business, including as features moderate hours of labour, safe and hygienic surroundings, with provision, proportioned at first to length of service, for sickness, accident and age. The beginnings of a national productive and distributive system for the supply of public employees, at cost and not for profit, would follow. It is confidently believed that the nationalizing of a single important service, by experience of the benefits in all the aspects mentioned resulting from it, will by its effect upon public opinion greatly hasten the full adoption of the system.

Seventh. The nationalizing and municipalizing of the businesses mentioned and of others will not, as has been alleged, bring a body of voters under the political control of government. It is an essential principle of Nationalism that in all departments of public business only the chiefs and heads of departments are to be subject to executive appointment or removal. As to the main body of the force, it is proposed that each service shall be strictly graded, with admissions only to the lowest grade. Such admissions shall not be by appointment, but in skilled employments vacancies shall be filled by candidates in the order of their fitness as shown by prescribed tests of qualifications, and in the case of unskilled employments not requiring special qualifications, by selection by lot from among applicants found generally qualified. Promotion is to be by record only, a matter of right and not of favour; removals to be only for cause, after a hearing before a board existing for the purpose, superiors having power to suspend subordinates pending enquiry. There is another sort of quite prevalent political intimidation to which, meanwhile, Nationalism will put an end so fast as it is applied to industry — that is, the intimidation of employees by private employers.

Eighth. Nationalism does not propose a paternal government, but its logical and practical antithesis, a cooperative administration for the benefit of equal partners. As a matter of propriety in the use of language, paternalism can only be ascribed to a government in proportion as it is non-popular, implying as the term does a relation of superiority and benevolence in the attitude of the government towards the people. Whatever errors of policy a popular government may fall into must be described by other terms than paternalism, inasmuch as their motives are not benevolence, but the supposed self-interest of the rulers themselves — that is, of the people. Nevertheless, there does exist in this country today, despite our popular form of government, an unprecedented and most intolerable form of paternalism, against which Nationalism is a protest and a revolt. I refer to the capitalist and corporate paternalism resulting from the modern concentration of capital, whereby a few score individuals and corporations determine, arbitrarily and without regard to natural laws, on what terms the people of the United States shall eat, drink and wherewithal they shall be clothed, what business they may do and what they may not, and whether they may do any at all, exercising by industrial and commercial methods a power in a hundred directions over the livelihood and concerns and very existence of the people, such as the most despotic government never dared assert, and which year by year and even month by month is becoming more complete and inevitable.

This sort of paternalism, or, if I may coin the word, step-paternalism, Nationalism would make an end of. These stepfathers of the people Nationalists would depose. In irreconcilable opposition alike to governmental and to capitalist paternalism, Nationalists contend that the people have come of age and should take their own business into their own hands.

Too much emphasis cannot be laid upon the fact that, setting wholly aside all moral, humane, Christian, industrial and economical arguments for national cooperation, it has become a strictly political necessity, as the only way possible whereby to preserve republican equality and popular institutions against the vast aggregations of capital which are mastering the country. Any government, especially any popular government, which tolerates such mighty subjects, must end by becoming their tool. The conflict now upon us between plutocracy and the republic is one compared with which the struggle between North and South was a superficial inflammation. The American people have overslept, but they are now awakening to the imminence and peril of the crisis. It is because Nationalism alone has proposed a plan whereby corporate power may be abolished while the advantages of concentrated capital are retained that it has met with popular acceptance. It is because the conditions of the problem admit of no other solution that its ultimate adoption may be safely predicted. If the republic is to survive, not merely in name but in reality, it can only be upon the industrial basis of national cooperation. Between plutocracy and Nationalism the election must finally be made. There is no third choice.

The Christian Union, November 13, 1890

WHY EVERY WORKING MAN
SHOULD BE A NATIONALIST

Nothing in the world is more certain than that every working man is bound to be a Nationalist just as soon as he gets it fairly into his head what Nationalism means, and what Nationalists are trying to do. To put the whole thing in a sentence, what we are driving at is to extend popular government, the rule of the people, to industry and commerce. That is to say, we want to give the people the same voice in the regulation and direction of the industrial and commercial machine which they already have in regard to the political machine.

Look a moment at the contrast between the way our political government is regulated, and the way in which our industrial and commercial system is administered. Our political system is democratic, that is to say, it is governed by the people. Every man, be he dull or clever, rich or poor, has the same voice in it. It is in fact a popular government. On the other hand, our industrial and commercial system, the productive and distributing machinery of the country, is not controlled by the people, nor have they any voice in it. A small number of individuals and groups of individuals own and run it purely for their own profit, without any authority from the people, or any responsibility to the people, and with no reference whatever to anybody's interests but their own. So we have, side by side, democracy in politics and despotism in industry and economics.

Now which is the more important to all of us who are not beyond the need of earning a living — to have a voice about the few and comparatively insignificant matters that belong to political administration, or to have a voice in governing the industrial system of production and distribution on which our livelihood depends? Can there possibly be two opinions about this? Is it not a sham and a lie to call a nation a republic, and a system democratic, in which the people are allowed once in four years to decide which of two politicians shall draw a fifty thousand dollar salary as president, but denied any voice at all in regulating the system of production and distribution on which depends all that makes life worth living?

That is what we Nationalists think and say, and what we want to do is to make this and every other nation a true republic, a real democracy, by bringing the entire business system of the country under the same popular government which now extends only to the few comparatively trifling functions called political.

Now you see exactly what we are aiming at in seeking to bring about the public operation of lighting plants, waterworks, tramways, ferries, canals, telegraphs, telephones, railroads, express service, coal mines and so on, indefinitely. These are all steps, small steps sometimes, but logical ones, towards the complete assertion of popular government over the entire field of production and distribution.

When this program is fulfilled there will be no private capitalists left to demand dividends or profits, and the proceeds of the national industries will be disposed of by the voice of the people, as the directors of the national corporation, and because the vote of all the directors will be equal it will follow that the dividend will have to be equal. That is to say the end of Nationalism will be the economic or wealth equality of all citizens; all being, on the other hand, required to render service according to their gifts and choice.

But are the weak and the women to share equally with the strong men? Most surely! It would never do to let the strong get the advantages of complete social cooperation while evading its duties. Even in the present imperfect system of society, this law of equal sharing in results, even though contributions are very unequal, is recognized in all the relations of the citizens to organized society. Taxes are paid in very unequal amounts, but are expended for the equal use of all. So military service in combines where it is universally required is rendered very unequally by men and not at all by women; yet all alike are equally entitled to the full military protection of the nation in case of need.

If you do not care to look so far ahead as to the full triumph of Nationalism, the immediate advantages of each step in its programme are plain and large enough to command your support, quite apart from the ultimate result. The substitution of public for private control of any business means at once its great cheapening, for public operation is quite or nearly at cost. The public operation of a business, moreover, at once makes a public official of every employee in it, and everybody knows that public employment in a republican country, as compared with private employment, means respectful treatment, reasonable hours, the best rates of pay and comparative security of position. It means, in fact, a management responsible to public opinion instead of the arbitrary rule of private capital aiming at profit only. Every business thus nationalized or municipalized is one more blow at the power which private capitalism exercises in the labour and goods markets and in legislative lobbies against the interests of the people at large, and working men in particular.

Organized capital is beating organized labour all along the line, but a vote for the public operation of monopolies is a club by which the working man can, and eventually will, defeat and overthrow organized capital, and it is the only weapon by which that end can be accomplished.

As we said at the outset, nothing in the world is more certain than that every working man is bound to become a Nationalist as soon as he clearly understands what Nationalism is.

Building Trades' Council Souvenir, April 1893

THE PROGRAMME OF
THE NATIONALISTS

I have been asked to give some account of Nationalism with a statement of its programme and of the first steps to be taken in the logical development of the plan, with especial reference to America, though it is of course to be observed that the economic situation in the United States differs from that in older nations only in the suddenness with which oppressive conditions have been developed which in Europe are of ancient standing.

Nationalism is economic democracy. It proposes to deliver society from the rule of the rich, and to establish economic equality by the application of the democratic formula to the production and distribution of wealth. It aims to put an end to the present irresponsible control of the economic interests of the country by capitalists pursuing their private ends, and to replace it by responsible public agencies acting for the general welfare. That is to say, it is proposed to harmonize the industrial and commercial system with the political, by bringing the former under popular government, as the latter has already been brought, to be administered as the political government is, by the equal voice of all for the equal benefit of all. As political democracy seeks to guarantee men against oppression exercised upon them by political forms, so the economic democracy of Nationalism would guarantee them against the much more numerous and grievous oppressions exercised by economic methods. The economic democracy of Nationalism is indeed the corollary and necessary supplement of political democracy, without which the latter must forever fail to secure to a people the equalities and liberties which it promises.

The conditions which justify the present Nationalist agitation, especially in America, may be broadly stated in brief terms.

It is certainly self-evident that the manner of the organization and administration of the economic system which regulates the production and distribution of wealth, whereupon not only the entire welfare but even the bare lives of all depend, is infinitely more important to a people than the manner in which any other part of their affairs is regulated. The economic system of the United States was formerly, and within the memory of men now living, one which offered a fairly free field to individual enterprise, with some opportunity for all to acquire a comfortable livelihood if not wealth; and in consequence of this fact, despite many inequalities of condition, a good degree of popular contentment has until recent times prevailed.

By an economic revolution unprecedented in scope and rapidity of movement, these former conditions have been within the time of one generation, and chiefly within twenty years, completely transformed. In place of a field of free competition with a fair opportunity for individual initiative in every direction, our economic system now presents the aspect of a centralized government, or group of governments, administered by great capitalists and combinations of capitalists, who monopolize alike the direction and the profits of the industries of the people.

Although the economic rulers who have thus crushed out individual enterprise in this country control interests incomparably more important to the people than are the functions exercised by the so-called political government, yet, while our political governors hold power only by delegation from the people, and are strictly accountable to them for its exercise, those rulers who administer the economic government of the country, and hold the livelihood of the people in their hands, are not elected or in any way delegated to do so by the people, and admit no accountability to them for the manner in which they exercise their power.

Scorning the decent hypocrisies by which other sovereigns have been wont to cloak their pretensions, the capitalists who have mastered our economic government do not justify their rule by pretending either the divine right of kings, the consent of the governed or even a benevolent intention towards their subjects. They claim no other title to power than their ability to suppress resistance, and expressly avow personal gain as the sole motive of their policy. In pursuance of this end the administration of the economic government of the country has been so conducted as to concentrate in the hands of an insignificant proportion of the people the bulk of the wealth which must furnish the general means of subsistence.

Fifty years ago, when, with the application of steam to machinery, the power of capital relatively to labour was suddenly multiplied, this country was held to be the ideal democracy of history on account of the prevailing equality in the distribution of wealth, and the general contentment and public spirit on the part of the people consequent thereon. At the present time thirty-one thousand men are reputed to possess one-half of the wealth upon which sixty-five million persons depend for existence, and the greater part of the other half is owned by a small additional fraction of the population, leaving the vast numerical majority of the nation without any considerable stake in the country. By the latest estimates, based upon the returns of the census of 1890, nine percent of the population of the United States owns seventy-one percent of the wealth of the country, leaving but twenty-nine percent to the remaining ninety-one percent of the population; and four thousand and seventy-four persons or families, being the richest group among the nine percent mentioned, own one-fifth of the total wealth of the country, or nearly as much as the aggregate holdings of ninety-one percent of the people.

History records no expropriation of a nation so complete as this, effected within so short a time, since the ages when military conquest meant the wholesale confiscation of the goods and persons of the conquered people. The population of Europe, indeed, groan under similar conditions, but with them they are the heritage of past ages, not, as in America, the result of an economic revolution effected within one lifetime.

This drainage of the nation's wealth to enrich a petty class has produced extraordinary social changes and portends more disastrous ones. Our farming population, constituting the bulk of the people, and in the past the most prosperous and contented portion, the main support of the republic in peace and war, has been converted by intolerable economic pressure, and the prospect of being reduced to the condition of a peasantry, into the most revolutionary class in the nation. The transformation in the conditions of the artisans has not been less disastrous. With the consolidation of capital in vast masses under corporate management, all that was humane in the relation of employer and employed has disappeared, and mutual suspicion and hatred and an attitude of organized hostility have taken their place. It has become the chief function of the militia to overawe strikers and suppress the disturbances of discontented working men. We are being taught by object-lessons of startling frequency that our industrial system, like the political systems of Europe, rests, in the end, upon the bayonet. The old-world caste distinctions of upper, lower and middle classes — terms abhorrent to our fathers — are being rapidly adopted among us, and mark only too justly the disintegration of our once integral and coherent communities into mutually embittered elements which the iron bands of political despotism will soon be needed to hold together in a state.

In view of this situation, which has resulted from the conquest and exploitation of our economic system by an irresponsible and despotic oligarchy, Nationalists maintain that if the people of the United States would retain any part of the high estate of equality, liberty and material welfare which formerly made them the world's envy, it is full time for them, in the exercise of their supreme power over governments and institutions, to make an end of the usurpation which has so imperilled their condition, and to establish in its place a new system of economic administration, "laying its foundations in such principles, and organizing its powers in such form, as shall to them seem most likely to effect their safety and happiness".

What sort of an industrial and economic government shall the people establish in place of the present irresponsible rule of the rich? The question answers itself to a certain extent; for, if the people establish the government, manifestly it must be a popular government. But another question remains. Shall this government be exercised by the people individually, or collectively? Shall we seek to restore the state of things which existed half a century and more ago, when independent individual enterprise was the rule in every field of industry and commerce, and a hundred competitive concerns did the business now attended to by one? Even if it were desirable to bring back that era, it would be as much out of the question as to restore the virgin continent, the boundless resources, the unoccupied lands and the other material conditions that made it possible.

The industrial system that is to employ and maintain our dense population, under the present and future conditions of the country, must be a systematized, centralized, interlocking economic organization of the highest efficiency. It is a physical impossibility to restore to the people, as individuals, the government of their economic interests; but it is feasible to bring it under their collective control, and that is the only possible alternative to economic oligarchy or, as it is called, plutocracy. This is the programme of Nationalism. We hold that the industrial system of a nation, like its political system, ought to be a government of the people, by the people, for the people, and for all of them equally. To that end we desire to see organized as public business all the industrial and commercial affairs of the people, so that they may be carried on henceforth, like all other public business, by responsible public agents, for the equal benefit of all citizens.

This plan is called Nationalism because it proceeds by the nationalization of industries, including, as minor applications of the same principle, the municipalization and state control of localized businesses.

Socialism implies the socializing of industry. This may or may not be based upon the national organism, and may or may not imply economic equality. As compared with socialism, Nationalism is a definition not in the sense of apposition or exclusion, but of a precision rendered necessary by a cloud of vague and disputed implications historically attached to the former word.

Perhaps the most common objection to the plan of nationalizing industry and carrying it on as public business is that it will involve more government. It is not so. Nationalization will simply substitute one sort of government for another. The industrial system which has grown up in the United States is, as we have shown, a government of the most rigid and despotic sort. In place of the irresponsible masters who now rule the economic interests of the people with a rod of iron, Nationalism will substitute popular self-government. Thomas Jefferson is quoted as saying that the government that governs least is self-government. That was what the signers of the American Declaration of Independence thought when they insisted on setting up a government of their own in spite of King George's willingness to manage their affairs for them. That is what Nationalists think in advocating popular government of the people's industrial interests in place of the present economic oligarchy.

It will tend to a clear understanding of the programme of Nationalism if we distinguish carefully between the features of the plan considered as fully carried out, and as in process of introduction. Many of the most certain and necessary consequences of Nationalism, when fully carried out, must remain till then quite impracticable. Among these is the principle of the indefeasible economic equality of all citizens, without regard, of course, to sex.

Economic equality is the obvious corollary of political equality as soon as the economic system is democratized. Quite apart from ethical considerations in its favour, it follows, as a matter of course, from the equal voice of all in determining the method of distribution. Whatever a democratic state undertakes must be undertaken for the common — that is, the equal — benefit of all. The European socialists, or a large part of them, do not insist upon economic equality, but allow economic variations in the ideal state. This is because they do not, like the Nationalists, deduce their conclusions by the rigid application of the democratic idea to the economic system. But while economic equality is the keystone of Nationalism, it must wait till the nation has fully organized its productive system. The arch must be finished before the keystone is placed, though after it is placed the stability of the arch depends upon it.

While Nationalists recognize as legitimate the demand for something definite in the way of a programme from a party of radical reform, it is not to be inferred that they pretend to forecast with exactness the course of events. Great revolutions, however peaceful they may be, do not follow prearranged plans, but make channels for themselves of which we may at best predict the general direction and outcome. Meanwhile, Nationalists would prepare the way by a step-by-step extension of the public conduct of business, which shall go as fast or as slow as public opinion may determine.

In making any industry or service public business, two ends should be kept equally in view, viz: first, the benefit of the public by more cheap, efficient and honest service or commodities; and second, but as an end in every way equally important, the immediate amelioration of the condition of workers taken over from private into public service. As to the first point, whenever a service or business is taken over to be publicly conducted, it should be managed strictly at cost; that is to say, the service or product should be furnished at the lowest cost that will pay the expense and proper charges of the business. Nationalism contemplates making all production for use and not for profit, and every nationalized business should be a step in that direction by eliminating profit so far as it is concerned.

As to the improvement in the condition of the workers, which is the other and equal end to be sought in all cases of nationalizing a business, it is enough to say that the state should show itself the model employer. Moderate hours of labour, healthful and safe conditions, with provisions for sickness, accident and old age, and a system for the admission, promotion and discharge of employees strictly based on merit, and absolutely exclusive of all capricious personal interference for political or other reasons, should characterize all publicly conducted business from the start. In particular cases, such as the clothing manufacture now so largely carried on by sweater's slaves, decent wages and conditions might temporarily raise the price of ready-made clothing. If it did it would only show how necessary it had been to make the business a state monopoly; and we may add that, on grounds of humanity, this is one of the first that should be brought under public management.

As to the general question as to the order in which different branches of business should be nationalized, or (which is the same thing) brought under municipal or state control, ownership and operation, Nationalists generally agree that chartered businesses of all sorts, which, as holding public franchises, are already quasi-public services, should first receive attention. Under this head come telegraphs and telephones, railroads both local and general, municipal lighting, waterworks, ferries and the like. The railroads alone employ some eight hundred thousand men, and the employees in the other businesses mentioned may raise that figure to one million, representing perhaps a total population of four million, certainly a rather big slice of the nation to begin with. These businesses would carry with them others. For example, the railroads are the largest consumers of iron and steel, and national operation of them would naturally carry with it the national operation of the larger part of the iron business. There are about five hundred thousand ironworkers in the country, implying a population of perhaps two million dependent on the industry, and making with the railroad and other employees and their dependents some six million persons. The same logic would apply to the mining of coal, with which, as carrier and chief consumer, the railroads are as closely identified.

The necessity of preserving what is left of our forests will soon force all the states to go into the forestry business, which may well be the beginning of public operation of the lumber industry. If our fast vanishing fisheries are to be protected, not merely national supervision, but national operation, will soon be necessary.

In the field of general business, the trusts and syndicates which have so largely stimulated the popular demand for Nationalism have also greatly simplified its progress. Whenever the managers of any department of industry or commerce have, in defiance of law and public interest, formed a monopoly, what is more just and proper than that the people themselves, through their agents, should take up and conduct the business in question at cost? In view of the fact that most of the leading branches of production have now been 'syndicated', it will be seen that this suggestion, fully carried out, would go far towards completing the plan of nationalization.

Meanwhile the same process would be going on upon other lines. Foreign governments which have large armies, in order to secure quality and cheapness, usually manufacture their soldiers' clothing, rations and various supplies in government factories. The British government, which is most like our own, was forced by the swindling of contractors to go into making clothing for the soldiers in the Crimean War, and has since kept it up with most admirable results. If our government had manufactured the soldiers' supplies in the Civil War, it would have saved a vast sum of money. It is highly desirable that it should forthwith begin to manufacture clothing and other necessaries for its soldiers and sailors, and for any other of its employees who might choose to be so served, as it is safe to say all would; for goods as represented, proof against adulteration and furnished at cost, would be a godsend even to a millionaire in these days of knavish trade. This policy of supplying the needs of government employees with the product of publicly conducted industries would bring about the whole productive and distributive plane of Nationalism in proportion as the number of employees increased.

Among special lines of business which ought at once to be brought under public management are the liquor traffic and fire and life insurance. It is proposed that every state should immediately monopolize the liquor traffic within its borders, and open places of sale in such localities as desire them. The liquors should be sold at cost — that is to say, at rates to pay all expenses of the system — by state agents, whose compensation should be fixed without relation, direct or indirect, to the amount of sales. This plan would eliminate desire of profit as a motive to stimulate sales, would ensure a strict regard to all conditions and requirements of law and would guarantee pure liquors. Pending the nationalization of the manufacture of liquors, the general government need be called on only for a transportation law protecting the states against illegal deliveries within their borders.

As to state life and fire insurance, this undertaking would need no plant and no backing save the state's credit on long-tested calculations of risks. It would be done at cost, in state buildings, by low-salaried officials, and without any sort of competitive or advertising expenses. This would mean a saving to fire insurers of at least twenty-five percent in premiums, and of at least fifty percent to life insurers, and would, above all, give insurance that was not itself in need of being reinsured.

When private plants are taken over by a city, state or nation, they should of course be paid for; the basis of valuation being the present cost of a plant of equal utility. Of course this subject of compensation should be considered in view of the fact that the ultimate effect of Nationalism will be the extinction of all economic superiorities, however derived.

The organization of the unemployed on a basis of state-supervised cooperation is an urgent undertaking in line with the programme of Nationalism. The unemployed represent a labour force which only lacks organization to be abundantly self-sustaining. It is the duty and interest of the state to so organize the unemployed, according to their several trades and aptitudes — the women workers as well as the men — that their support shall be provided for out of their own product, which should not go upon the market for sale, but be wholly consumed within the circle of the producers, thus in no way deranging outside prices or wages. This plan contemplates the unemployed problem as being a permanent one, with periods of special aggravation, and as therefore demanding for its solution a permanent and elastic provision for a circle of production and consumption complete in itself and independent of the commercial system. There is no other method for dealing with the unemployed problem which does not mock it.

In proportion as the industries, commerce and general business of the country are publicly organized, the source of the power and means of the growth of the plutocracy, which depend upon the control and revenues of industry, will be undermined and cut off. In the same measure, obviously, the regulation of the employment of the people and the means of providing for their maintenance will pass under their collective control. To complete the plan of Nationalism by carrying out its guarantee of equal maintenance to all with employment according to fitness will require only a process of systematization and equalizing of conditions under an already unified administration.

The work of Nationalists has hitherto been chiefly educational. This must necessarily have been the case from the magnitude of the scheme, requiring, as it does, something like national acceptance for the undertaking of its larger features. In the department, especially, of local public services, such as waterworks, lighting, transit and the like, something like a wave of feeling in favour of the municipalization of such undertakings has within three years swept over the country, and, far from subsiding, is swelling into a tide. In nearly every progressive community there has sprung up within a few years a more or less strong nucleus of citizens which meets every fresh oppression of chartered corporations with the demand for public operation. The insolent taunt of entrenched monopoly — "What are you going to do about it?" — no longer strikes the people dumb. An answer is on every lip, and it is — Nationalism! The sudden recent advance in the first rank among the topics of the day, in the news and periodical press, of the questions of the public operation of commerce and business as a remedy for capitalistic abuse is of course the best general evidence of the extent to which the public mind is occupied with this subject.

Doubtless, however, the most startling single demonstration of the rapidity and solidity of the growth of Nationalism is the fact that in the presidential campaign of 1892 more than one million votes were polled for the People's Party, the platform of which embodied the most important features of the immediate Nationalist programme as above stated. That even this platform was not radical enough to satisfy a large portion of the party and its sympathizers has been made evident by the far more advanced ground taken subsequently by state and local conventions, by the great labour organizations in their national and local assemblies, and by the Farmer's Alliances. Indeed, the statement may be safely made that, so far as the economic and industrial discontent in this country has hitherto found definite expression, it has taken the form of demands for the more or less complete application of the nationalization idea to business. This is simply because there is found to be, upon examination, no other way out.

Persons whose minds are first directed to Nationalism often miss the point by failing to see that it is inevitable as the only alternative of plutocracy, if the latter is not to triumph. Such persons are wont to regard the nationalization or public conduct of industry as merely one economic device among many, to be compared with the rest as more or less attractive or ingenious. They fail to perceive that it is the necessary and only method by which a solution of the economic question can be secured which shall be democratic in character. Many who sincerely believe — or think they do — in popular government and the democratic idea as a general principle would doubtless see this question differently if they took time to consider that by the very meaning of the terms the public management of industry is the substitution of popular for class and personal government, and that in opposing it they stand squarely against the democratic idea and in favour of oligarchical rule in the most extensive and important department of human interests.

There are two principles on which the blended affairs of human beings in society may be regulated: Government by all for all, and Government by a few for a few. The time is at hand when it is to be determined whether the one principle or the other shall henceforth regulate the organization of human labour and the distribution of its fruits. The countless past combats in the immemorial struggle of the many against the few, whether for personal, religious or political liberty, have but cleared the way and led up to this all-embracing, all-concluding issue, now being joined the world over. It is the decisive battle to which all the former engagements were but preliminary skirmishes.

Not in many ages, surely — perhaps never — have men and women, during their brief probations on earth, had an opportunity to make so momentous a mistake as those will who take the wrong side in this battle.

The Forum, March 1894

FOURTH OF JULY, 1992

I n the year 1992, it is safe to say, the Fourth of July will have ceased to be a popular holiday of much note. Somewhere between today and the Fourth of July, 1992, there will be another Declaration of Independence in America which, in importance, will quite eclipse the document (great in its way as that was) which was promulgated at Philadelphia one hundred and sixteen years ago.

Our descendants, as intelligent students of history, will no doubt give due recognition to the work done that day as a necessary step in the national evolution, but they will not the less marvel in their hearts at the exceeding simplicity of a people who could consider themselves free and independent, merely because as states they had sundered certain political ties with a foreign state, while retaining for the regulation of their mutual relations as individuals an economic system based on inequalities of wealth which made the many dependants and suppliants of the few for all the means of life and happiness, and even for the opportunity to stand upon the earth and toil.

The new declaration of independence which I predict will not deal with the relations of this country with other countries, but with the relations of the people of this country with one another.

It will abolish for all time the distinctions of mastership and servitude, employer and employed, capitalist and proletarian, and declare every man forevermore independent of every other man and every woman of every man.

It will put an end to economic inequality as the root of all injustice and proclaim the industrial republic wherein all the citizens shall be equal cooperators in producing the means of life and enjoyment and equal sharers in the results.

On what day of what month of what year this new and greater declaration of independence will come I am not so presumptuous as to predict, but I believe it will come and that society will be, peaceably or forcibly, conformed to its terms within the expectation of life of men now middle-aged.

Seeing then that our present little Fourth of July is so soon to pass into comparative obscuration, let us make the most of it while we have it, piously remembering that had not our fathers worked the deliverance they did in their day, their posterity would not be able to work the greater deliverance that is now at hand.

Boston Globe, July 4, 1892

HOW I WROTE
"LOOKING BACKWARD"

U p to the age of eighteen I had lived almost continually in a thriving village of New England, where there were no very rich and very few poor, and everybody who was willing to work was sure of a fair living. At that time I visited Europe and spent a year there in travel and study. It was in the great cities of England, Europe and among the hovels of the peasantry that my eyes were first fully opened to the extent and consequences of man's inhumanity to man.

I well remember in those days of European travel how much more deeply that blue background of misery impressed me than the palaces and cathedrals in relief against it. I distinctly recall the innumerable debates, suggested by the piteous sights about us, which I had with a dear companion of my journey, as to the possibility of finding some great remedy for poverty, some plan for equalizing human conditions. Our discussions usually brought up against the same old stump: Who would do the dirty work? We did not realize, as probably few do who lightly dismiss the subject of social reform with the same query, that its logic implies the condonation of all forms of slavery. Not until we all acknowledge the world's 'dirty work' as our common and equal responsibility shall we be in a position intelligently to consider, or have the disposition seriously to seek, a just and reasonable way of distributing and adjusting the burden. So it was that I returned home, for the first time aroused to the existence and urgency of the social problem, but without as yet seeing any way out. Although it had required the sights of Europe to startle me to a vivid realization of the inferno of poverty beneath our civilization, my eyes having once been opened I had now no difficulty in recognizing in America, and even in my own comparatively prosperous village, the same conditions in course of progressive development.

The other day rummaging among old papers I was much interested by the discovery of some writings indicative of my state of mind at that period. If the reader will glance over the following extracts from the manuscript of an address which it appears I delivered before the Chicopee Falls Village Lyceum along in 1871 or 1872, he will probably admit that their youthful author was quite likely to attempt something in the line of "Looking Backward" if he only lived long enough. The subject of this address was "The Barbarism of Society", the barbarism being held to consist in and result from inequality in the distribution of wealth. From numerous equally radical expressions I excerpt these paragraphs:

> The great reforms of the world have hitherto been political rather than social. In their progress classes privileged by title have been swept away, but classes privileged by wealth remain. A nominal aristocracy is ceasing to exist, but the actual aristocracy of wealth, the world over, is every day becoming more and more powerful. The idea that men can derive a right from birth or name to dispose of the destinies of their fellows is exploded, but the world thinks not yet of denying that gold confers a power upon its possessors to domineer over their equals and enforce from them a life's painful labours at the price of a bare subsistence. I would not have indignation blind my eyes or confuse my reason in the contemplation of this injustice, but I ask you what is the name of an institution by which men control the labour of other men, and out of the abundance created by that labour having doled out to the labourers such a pittance as may barely support life and sustain strength for added tasks, reserve to themselves the vast surplus for the support of a life of ease and splendour? This, gentlemen, is slavery; a slavery whose prison is the world, whose shackles and fetters are the unyielding frame of society, whose lash is hunger, whose taskmasters are those bodily necessities for whose supply the rich who hold the keys of the world's granaries must be appealed to, and the necks of the needy bowed to their yoke as the price of the boon of life. . . .
>
> Consider a moment the condition of that class of society by whose unremitting toil the ascendancy of man over the material universe is maintained and his existence rendered possible on earth, remembering, also,

that this class comprises the vast majority of the race. Born of parents whom brute passion impelled to the propagation of their kind; bred in penury and the utter lack of all those luxuries and amenities of life which go so far to make existence tolerable; their intellectual faculties neglected and an unnatural and forced development given to their basest instincts; their childhood, the sweet vacation of life, saddened and deadened by the pinching of poverty, and then, long before the immature frame could support the severity of labour, forced from the playground into the factory or field! Then begins the obscure, uninteresting drama of a labourer's life; an unending procession of toilsome days relieved by brief and rare holidays and harassed by constant anxiety lest he lose all he claims from the world — a place to labour. He feels, in some dumb, unreasoning way, oppressed by the frame of society, but it is too heavy for him to lift. The institutions that crush him down assume to his dulled brain the inevitable and irresistible aspect of natural laws. And so, with only that dim sense of injustice which no subtlety of reasoning, no array of argument, can banish from the human soul when it feels itself oppressed, he bows his head to his fate.

Let not anyone falsely reply that I am dreaming of a happiness without toil, of abundance without labour. Labour is the necessary condition, not only of abundance but of existence upon earth. I ask only that none labour beyond measure that others may be idle, that there be no more masters and no more slaves among men. Is this too much? Does any fearful soul exclaim, impossible, that this hope has been the dream of men in all ages, a shadowy and Utopian reverie of a divine fruition which the earth can never bear? That the few must revel and the many toil; the few waste, the many want; the few be masters, the many serve; the toilers of the earth be the poor and the idlers the rich, and that this must go on forever?

Ah, no; has the world then dreamt in vain. Have the ardent longings of the lovers of men been towards an unattainable felicity? Are the aspirations after liberty, equality and happiness implanted in the very core of our

hearts for nothing?
Not so, for nothing that is unjust can be eternal and
nothing that is just can be impossible.

Since I came across this echo of my youth and recalled the
half-forgotten exercises of mind it testifies to, I have been
wondering, not why I wrote "Looking Backward", but why I did
not write it, or try to, twenty years ago.
Like most men, however, I was under the sordid and selfish
necessity of solving the economic problem in its personal bearings
before I could give much time to the cure of society in general. I
had, like others, to fight my way to a place at the world's
work-bench where I could make a living. For a dozen or fifteen
years I followed journalism, doing in a desultory way, as
opportunity offered, a good deal of magazine and book writing. In
none of the writings of this period did I touch on the social
question, but not the less all the while it was in mind, as a problem
not by any means given up, how poverty might be abolished and
the economic equality of all citizens of the republic be made as
much a matter of course as their political equality. I had always
the purpose, sometime when I had sufficient leisure, to give myself
earnestly to the examination of this great problem, but meanwhile
kept postponing it, giving my time and thoughts to easier tasks.
Possibly I never should have mustered up courage for an
undertaking so difficult and indeed so presumptuous, but for
events which gave the problem of life a new and more solemn
meaning to me. I refer to the birth of my children.
I confess I cannot understand the mental operations of good
men or women who from the moment they are parents do not
become intensely interested in the social question. That an
unmarried man or even a man childless though married should
concern himself little about the future of a race in which he may
argue that he will have no personal stake is conceivable, though
such indifference is not morally edifying.
From the time their children are born it becomes the great
problem with parents how to provide for and safeguard their
future when they themselves shall no longer be on earth. To this
end they painfully spare and save and plot and plan to secure for
their offspring all the advantages that may give them a better
chance than other men's children in the struggle for existence.

They do this, knowing sadly well the while, from observation and experience, how vain all such safeguards may prove, how impossible it is for even the wisest and wealthiest of fathers to make sure that the cherished child he leaves behind may not be glad to earn his bread as a servant to the children of his father's servants. Still the parent toils and saves, feeling that this is the best and all he can do for his offspring, little though it be. But is it? Surely a moment's thought will show that this is a wholly unscientific way of going about the work of providing for the future of one's children.

This is the problem of all problems to which the individualistic method is most inapplicable, the problem before all others of which the only adequate solution must necessarily be a social solution. Your fear for your child is that he may fall into the ditch of poverty or be waylaid by robbers. So you give him a lantern and provide him with arms. That would be all very well if you could not do better, but would it not be an infinitely wiser and more efficient method to join hands with all the other equally anxious parents, and fill up the ditch and exterminate the robbers, so that safety might be a matter of course for all? However high, however wise, however rich you are, the only way you can surely safeguard your child from hunger, cold and wretchedness, and all the deprivations, degradations and indignities which poverty implies, is by a plan that will equally safeguard all men's children. This principle once recognized, the solution of the social problem becomes a simple matter. Until it is, no solution is possible.

According to my best recollection it was in the fall or winter of 1886 that I sat down to my desk with the definite purpose of trying to reason out a method of economic organization by which the republic might guarantee the livelihood and material welfare of its citizens on a basis of equality corresponding to and supplementing their political equality. There was no doubt in my mind that the proposed study should be in the form of a story. This was not merely because that was a treatment which would command greater popular attention than others. In adventuring in any new and difficult field of speculation I believe that the student often cannot do better than to use the literary form of fiction. Nothing outside of the exact sciences has to be so logical as the thread of a story, if it is to be acceptable. There is no such test of a false and absurd idea as trying to fit it into a story. You may make a sermon or an essay or a philosophical treatise as illogical as you please and no one know the difference, but all the world is a good critic of a story, for it has to conform to the laws of ordinary probability and commonly observed sequence, of which we are all judges.

The stories that I had written before "Looking Backward" were largely of one sort, namely, the working out of problems, that is to say, attempts to trace the logical consequences of certain assumed conditions. It was natural, therefore, that in this form the plan of "Looking Backward" should present itself to my mind. Given the United States, a republic based upon the equality of all men and conducted by their equal voice, what would the natural and logical way be by which to go about the work of guaranteeing an economic equality to its citizens corresponding with their political equality, but without the present unjust discrimination of sex? From the moment the problem first clearly presented itself to my mind in this way, the writing of the book was the simplest thing in the world.

"Looking Backward" has been frequently called a 'fanciful' production. Of course, the notion of a man's being resuscitated after a century's sleep is fanciful, and so, of course, are the various other whimsies about life in the year 2000 necessarily inserted to give colour to the picture. The argument of the book is, however, about as little fanciful as possible. It is, as I have said, an attempt to work out logically the results of regulating the national system of production and distribution by the democratic principle of the equal rights of all, determined by the equal voice of all.

I defend as material no feature of the plan which cannot be shown to be in accord with that method.

Many excellent persons, not without sympathy with the idea of a somewhat more equal distribution of this world's wealth, have objected to the principle of absolute and invariable economic equality underlying the plan developed in "Looking Backward". Many have seemed to think that here was an arbitrary detail that might just as well have been modified by admitting economic inequality in proportion to unequal values of industrial service. So it might have been if the plan had been the fanciful theory they supposed it, but regarding it as the result of a rigid application of the democratic idea to the economic system, no feature of the whole plan is more absolutely a matter of course, a more logical necessity, than just that. Political equality, which gives all citizens an equal voice in government, without regard to the great differences between men as to intelligence, public service, personal worth and wealth, is the recognition that the essential dignity of human nature is of an importance transcending all personal attributes and accidents and is, therefore, not to be limited by them. In applying the democratic idea to the economic organization, economic equality, without regard to differences of industrial ability, is necessitated by precisely the same logic which justifies political equality. The two ideas are one and stand or fall together.

Nor is economic equality any more an ethical than a necessary physical consequence of democratic rule extended to the productive and distributive system. Political equals will never legislate economic inequality. Nor should they do so. Self-preservation forbids it, for economic inequality presently undermines and nullifies political equality and every other form of equality as well.

Moreover, under any system proportioning wealth distribution to industrial performance, how could women be assured an indefeasible equality with men, and their yoke of economic dependence upon the other sex with all its related and implied subserviences, be finally broken? Surely no social solution not securely guaranteeing that result could claim to be adequate.

I have stopped by the way to say these few words about the plan of "Looking Backward" as the result of the rigid application of the democratic formula to the social problem, and concerning the feature of absolute economic equality as a necessary effect of that method, because it is in these points and their implications that Nationalism, as suggested by "Looking Backward", is, perhaps, most strongly differentiated from other socialistic solutions.

As to the form of the story, my first notion was, while keeping the resuscitated man as a link between the two centuries, not to make him the narrator, or to write chiefly from his point of view, but rather from that of the twentieth century. This would have admitted of some very interesting effects and about half the story was at first written on that line, but as I became convinced of the practical availability of the social solution I was studying, it became my aim to sacrifice all other effects to the method which would enable me to explain its features most fully, which was manifestly that of presenting everything from the point of view of the representative of the nineteenth century.

I have been very frequently asked if I anticipated any considerable effect from the publication of "Looking Backward", and whether I was not very much surprised at the sensation it produced. I cannot say that I was surprised. If it be asked what was the basis of my expectations, I answer the effect of the writing of the book upon myself. When I first undertook to work out the results of a democratic organization of production and distribution based on the recognition of an equal duty of individual service by all citizens and an equal share by all in the result, according to the analogies of military service and taxation and all other relations between the state and the citizen, I believed, indeed, it might be possible on this line to make some valuable suggestions upon the social problem, but it was only as I proceeded with the enquiry that I became fully convinced of the entire adequacy of the principle as a social solution, and, moreover, that the achievement of this solution was to be the next great step in human evolution. It would, indeed, be a most impassive person in whose mind so mighty a hope could grow without producing strong emotions.

Knowing that "as face answereth to face in water, so the heart of man to man", I could not doubt that the hope that moved me must needs, in like manner, move all who should come even in part to share it.

As well as I can remember, "Looking Backward" began in earnest to be written in the fall or winter of 1886, and was substantially finished in the following six or eight months, although rewriting and revising took up the following spring and summer. It went to the publishers in August or September, 1887, and although promptly accepted did not appear till January, 1888. Although it made a stir among the critics up to the close of 1888, the sales had not exceeded ten thousand, after which they leaped into the hundred thousands.

INTRODUCTION TO
"THE FABIAN ESSAYS"

The introduction to the American public of the present
edition of the deservedly famous English work known as
"The Fabian Essays" is an occasion that suggests some
general observations upon the subject of socialism, considered
especially from the American point of view.

Until very recently socialism has been a word rarely heard in the
United States, and still more rarely understood, even among
intelligent persons. Till quite lately the average American has
conceived of a socialist, when he has considered him at all, as a
mysterious type of desperado, reputed to infest the dark places of
continental Europe and engaged with his fellows in a conspiracy
as monstrous as it was futile against civilization and all that it
implied. That such an atrocious and hopeless undertaking should
find any following of sane men has seemed accountable only by
the oppressions of European despots and their maddening effect
on the popular mind. That socialism could never take root in a
republic like ours was assumed as an axiom. Though it might be
well enough for Americans to study the phenomena of socialism,
in a philosophic and purely speculative way, as a disease of
monarchical systems, anyone would have been laughed at who
should have suggested ten years ago that the subject would ever
have a practical interest to our people.

That was but yesterday, and today the most significant and
important movement of thought among the American people is
agreed by all observers to be the growth of the socialistic
sentiment. Today, in this country, the various aspects of radical
social and economic reform on socialistic lines are the most
prominent themes of literary treatment, of public discussion, and
of private debate whenever two or three serious-minded persons
take counsel together as to the state of the nation.

At first, when the social question so suddenly seized upon the
attention of the American people, there were those who reasoned
that the interest in the subject would prove transient; that it was,

in fact, but a 'fad'. There are few, if any, who so delude themselves at this writing. So rapidly has the popular interest in socialistic ideas broadened and deepened, and shown its working in the fields of literature, of legislation, of political organization, that there are today few so purblind as not to see and admit that the social problem, the great problem of social justice here, as in Europe, can be got rid of only by being solved, and, until then, will have no mercy on our peace. Already it is apparent from the shaping of events that the public questions of the coming time are to be social, industrial, humane, and not political and partisan. They are to be concerned, not with the external relations of the nation with other nations, but with the radical analysis and reconstruction of the relations in which classes and individuals within the nation stand towards one another and the whole. More and more all other issues are to be subordinated to and absorbed in the one great issue between the present economic system, on the one hand, and a radically new and nobler system on the other. In this great controversy we all who yet have any considerable stretch of life before us must take one side or the other, and the air already is electric with the tension of decision. The elderly men who are about retiring from the stage of public affairs may be able without too much discredit, provided they are not dilatory, to carry to the grave intact the ignorance of their generation as to socialism, but no branch of education is going to be more essential to the outfit of the rising generation than a full and discriminating acquaintance with the subject. These are conditions surely which leave no argument necessary as to the public utility of all efforts at the present time to promote the study, by Americans especially, of socialism or, if we may so translate the term, of humane economics, as contrasted with the political economy of the schools.

At the outset of any such study several general questions are suggested. What is socialism? Why is it so late a comer among the forces of civilization? For while so very newly arisen in America, it has really not been known very much longer (only some fifty years or so) in Europe. Why again has it come to the front at this particular time in America, and why did it raise its head earlier in Europe? And why have its ideas never in previous ages produced any deep or extended movement among the nations of the world?

For the purpose of these questions socialism may be said to be the application of the democratic method to the economic administration of a people. It aims by substituting public management of industry and commerce in the common interest, for private management in diverse personal interests, to more nearly equalize the distribution of wealth, while at the same time increasing the volume of wealth produced for distribution. This definition, while, of course, not going at all into details, will suffice to suggest the answer to the second question raised, namely why has socialism been so late a comer among the forces of civilization? It is simply because the democratic idea — the idea of self-government by the people for their own benefit — has only within a very recent period achieved a firm establishment in men's minds. The democratic idea must first be established as a general theory of government, that is, in the political field, before the idea can occur of applying it to the economic field. The democratic movement in Europe, although the French Revolution broke the ground for it, did not effectively begin till the first third and middle of the present century, after the reaction against the Revolution had lost its force. Consequently, we find, as might be expected, the rise of socialism dating from that period. European democracy, almost from the first, took on a socialistic quality for the reason that the pressing economic misery of the people suggested as most urgent the application of the new popular power to the economic problem. We also find suggested in this statement the explanation of the fact that although democracy in politics was established in America a century before it began to make serious progress in Europe, yet in the Old World the socialistic idea originated fifty years before it began to stir here. Socialism results spontaneously when a people having a pressing economic problem to deal with become masters of the democratic method. In Europe the problem was already there and had been for ages, when the method first came to hand. In America we had the method of solution but lacked, until recently, any pressing economic problem to solve. Now the problem has come, and the Kansas farmer and the New England wage-earner, as they bring to its solution the democratic methods they have so long used for other purposes, become in a day socialists, without having ever before heard of socialism.

Up to within a recent period, owing to our scanty population and vast resources, the question of a comfortable subsistence has been in America one which every tolerably energetic person has been fairly well able to solve for himself. So great has been the plenty, that the individualistic "every man for himself and the devil for the hindmost" way of getting a living — crude, wasteful, brutal as it was — nevertheless sufficed to secure a good degree of general comfort and an approximate equality of fortunes. This period has now come to an end. Within the past few decades, the concentration of wealth in the hands of a few has been proceeding at a rate, ever growing swifter, which now threatens a practical expropriation of the people in the interest of a small class. Indeed, it may almost be said that this expropriation has already been practically accomplished, for it has been shown by direct deductions from the mortgage statistics of the 1890 census that seventy-one percent of the aggregate wealth of the nation is already held by nine percent of the population, the remaining ninety-one percent of the population being limited to twenty-nine percent of the total wealth. It is further shown that four thousand and seventy-four American families, out of a total of thirteen million families, own twenty percent of this national wealth total, or two-thirds as much as belong to the ninety-one percent of the population mentioned above.

With such facts and figures to justify his growing sense of economic distress and oppression, the American must indeed be of sluggish mind who does not recognize already preparing for him, and in course of being fitted to his shoulders, the yoke of economic servitude his European brothers so long have borne. When we reflect that the population thus suddenly and unmistakably confronted with the prospect of degradation to servile and proletarian conditions is the proudest-spirited, the most generally intelligent ever known, with the sentiment of equality bred in the very bones, shall we wonder at the suddenness of the socialistic outburst in the United States, or the swift movement of its propaganda? Must we not rather recognize in the American situation conditions which justify the belief that the suddenness and swiftness of the rise of socialism in this country presage lusty vigour of growth which shall put America in her proper place as the world's pioneer in the pursuit of economic, as formerly of political, equality? May we not reasonably expect that the American people, having been confronted with the failure of the present economic system to secure human welfare even under the most favourable conditions, will display in the reconstruction of the economic fabric all that energy, that ingenuity and originality of device, and that rapidity of execution which are the distinguishing national characteristics?

Meanwhile, owing to the fact that, for the reasons stated, the social economic problem came earlier to the front in Europe than here, Americans have the advantage of a considerable body of foreign literature, German, French and English, devoted to the subject. Perhaps there is no single work in this socialistic library which is calculated to be more useful to the American reader who desires to obtain without laborious research a general knowledge of the argument for socialism than "The Fabian Essays". This is partly because of their popular style; partly from the excellent arrangement of the matter, with a view to giving an all-around idea of the subject, respectively from the historic, economic and moral viewpoints; and also in part from the degree of resemblance which obtains between English and American institutions and habits of thought. The fact that the essays are by different authors, each writing in a different style, has an effect to impart a pleasing variety, while the system with which the essays have been grouped secures an effect of coherency and method as satisfactory as could well have been gained by a single authorship. The arrangement of the contents has the further advantage, greatly assisted by the admirable index, of enabling the reader who does not care to read a book in course to select particular topics for study as his interest may incline. It is a pleasure especially to commend the good-tempered and reasonable tone which marks the argument of these writers. This method, it is needless to say, far from implying any compromising of the truth, lends itself to a more clear and incisive criticism of existing institutions than is consistent with violent and denunciatory rhetoric. The use of this argumentative method, which may be described as *suaviter in modo fortiter in re,* is indeed as characteristic of the Fabian Society in England as of the Nationalists in the United States.

But it may be that some reader may not know what this Fabian Society exactly is which gives its name to this volume and of which the essayists all are members. For the information of any such it may be said that the name was assumed a number of years ago by an organization of cultured Englishmen who, while devoted to a radical socialistic propaganda, believed that they could most effectually promote it by educational methods addressed to the reason rather than the prejudices of the community. In this view they have since been carrying on in England a very extensive and effective work, through tracts, books and, above all, popular lectures, the essays in this volume being indeed but specimens of these popular lectures revised for publication. While the more revolutionary English socialists make a show of deriding as too merely academic the propaganda of the Fabians, it may be doubted if work more valuable has ever been done by any socialist organization.

In addition to the essays contained in the English edition, the present volume includes a valuable and important additional feature in the form of a lecture of "The Fabian Society and Its Work", delivered in Boston by Mr. William Clarke, M.A., himself a Fabian and one of these essayists, in the winter of 1893-94, and afterwards published in the *New England Magazine.*

Nationalism is the form under which socialism has thus far been chiefly brought to the notice of the American people; and it is proper in a preface of this character to say a few words by way of explaining the relative significance of the terms. A socialist is one who believes that industry and commerce, on which the welfare of all depends, should not be left, as now, to be controlled irresponsibly by individuals for their private gain, but should be organized by the community, to be cooperatively conducted, with an equitable (not necessarily equal) distribution of the product among the members of the community. That is what socialism strictly means, and is all the creed that a socialist can be held to. Now it is a great deal to be able to subscribe to this creed, but it is not quite enough of a creed according to Nationalists. The criticism of the present system involved in it is adequate; but in defining the system of cooperation that is to take its place, it leaves unsettled the most vital point of that or any other industrial system, namely, the principle on which the industrial product is to be shared, for to say that the principle of the division is to be 'equitable' is no more than to say it should be reasonable, and leaves the whole question open to discussion. There is no standard to determine what an equitable division of anything is, if once we admit it may be an unequal division. The political economists, indeed, argue that the present division of wages and profits is really equitable, although so unequal. Now Nationalists are socialists who, holding all that socialists agree on, go further, and hold also that the distribution of the cooperative product among the members of the community must be not merely equitable, whatever that term may mean, but must be always and absolutely equal.

Of course it is not meant that many socialists are not believers in economic equality, but only that the creed of socialism does not of necessity imply it. Among the essayists in the present volume, Mrs. Besant, and probably others, seem strongly inclined towards the principle of equality, but that cannot be said, hitherto, of the general body of European socialists. The more general opinion among them appears to be that the ownership of the means of production should indeed be communal, but that the product should be apportioned among the workers in the same and in different occupations according to the relative value of their services, as if that could ever be satisfactorily or even practically adjusted under a non-competitive system.

This would leave the individual, as now, to be well-to-do or to want, according to his strength or weakness, and keep alive, although in much less glaring contrast, the economic distinctions of this day. Nationalists, on the other hand, would absolutely abolish these distinctions, and the possibility of their again arising, by making an equal provision for the maintenance of all an incident and an indefeasible condition of citizenship, without any regard whatever to the relative specific services of different citizens. The rendering of such services, on the other hand, instead of being left to the option of the citizen with the alternative of starvation, would be required under a uniform law as a civic duty, precisely like other forms of taxation or military service, levied on the citizen for the furtherance of a commonweal in which each is to share equally. This is called Nationalism, not in any narrow tribal sense opposed to universal fraternity, but because it consists in applying to the economic organization the idea exemplified in all national or public functions when undertaken in democratic or even in the progressive class of monarchical states.

All such public functions are supported either by tax or personal service, of the citizens, or both. The obligation of that service of tax or person is enforced by a uniform levy, but the amount of tax or service rendered under that levy is very unequal, depending on ability. This inequality of service is not, however, allowed to prejudice the right of all citizens to claim an equal benefit from all national or public expenditure or action. The rule of the state in coordinating the efforts of its members for any public purpose is the equal distribution of benefits resulting from necessarily unequal but uniformly levied contributions. So it must be when the nation assumes the organization of industry. The law of service must be uniform, but the services rendered will vary greatly — with many entire exemptions — according to the abilities of the people. The inequality of contributions will in no way prejudice the invariable law of equal distribution of the resultant sum.

It is confidently believed that all socialists will ultimately be led by the logic of events to recognize, as many now do, that the attitude of the Nationalists on this point is the only true socialistic one.

American Edition, 1894

INSTITUTE OF WORLD CULTURE

DECLARATION

To explore the classical and renaissance traditions of East and West and their continuing relevance to emerging modes and patterns of living

To renew the universal vision behind the American Dream through authentic affirmations of freedom, excellence and self-transcendence in an ever-evolving Republic of Conscience

To honour through appropriate observance the contributions of men and women of all ages to world culture

To enhance the enjoyment of the creative artistry and craftsmanship of all cultures

To deepen awareness of the universality of man's spiritual striving and its rich variety of expression in the religions, philosophies and literatures of humanity

To promote forums for fearless inquiry and constructive dialogue concerning the frontiers of science, the therapeutics of self-transformation, and the societies of the future

To investigate the imaginative use of the spiritual, mental and material resources of the globe in the service of universal welfare

To examine changing social structures in terms of the principle that a world culture is greater than the sum of its parts and to envision the conditions, prospects and possibilities of the world civilization of the future

To assist in the emergence of men and women of universal culture, capable of continuous growth in non-violence of mind, generosity of heart and harmony of soul

To promote universal brotherhood and to foster human fellowship among all races, nations and cultures

The Institute of World Culture, founded on July 4, 1976 *(Bicentennial)*, has launched influential publications to generate a continuing inquiry into the prospects and possibilities, the conditions and requirements, of the world civilization of the future. Current publications include analyses of contemporary social structures, contributions to philosophic and literary thought, as well as classic reprints from Plato, ancient Indian psychology, Edward Bellamy and Leo Tolstoy. They invite the reader to rethink and renew a vital sense of participation in the global inheritance of humanity and the emerging cosmopolis.

The Society of the Future
Raghavan Iyer

The Religion of Solidarity
Edward Bellamy

The Banquet
Plato

The Dream of Ravan
From *The Dublin University Magazine*

The Law of Violence and the Law of Love
Leo Tolstoy

The Recovery of Innocence
Pico Iyer

Utilitarianism and All That
Raghavan Iyer

Novus Ordo Seclorum
Raghavan Iyer

1407 Chapala Street
Santa Barbara, CA 93101

THE PYTHAGOREAN SANGHA

THE JEWEL IN THE LOTUS edited by Raghavan Iyer

THE GRIHASTHA ASHRAMA by B. P. Wadia

THE MORAL AND POLITICAL THOUGHT
OF MAHATMA GANDHI by Raghavan Iyer

THE PYTHAGOREAN ACADEMY

PARAPOLITICS — TOWARD THE CITY OF MAN by Raghavan Iyer

THE PLATONIC QUEST by E. J. Urwick

OBJECTIVITY AND CONSCIOUSNESS by Robert Rein'l

SANGAM TEXTS

THE BEACON LIGHT by H. P. Blavatsky

THE SERVICE OF HUMANITY by D. K. Mavalankar

HIT THE MARK by W. Q. Judge

THE PROGRESS OF HUMANITY by A. P. Sinnett

CONSCIOUSNESS AND IMMORTALITY by T. Subba Row

THE GATES OF GOLD by M. Collins

THE LANGUAGE OF THE SOUL by R. Crosbie

THE ASCENDING CYCLE by G. W. Russell

THE DOCTRINE OF THE BHAGAVAD GITA by Bhavani Shankar

THE LAW OF SACRIFICE by B. P. Wadia

SACRED TEXTS

The CGP emblem identifies this book as a production of Concord Grove Press, publishers since 1975 of books and pamphlets of enduring value in a format based upon the Golden Ratio. This volume was typeset in Times Roman, printed and softbound by Sangam Printers. A list of publications can be obtained from Concord Grove Press, P.O. Box 959, Santa Barbara, California 93102 U.S.A.